**BMW:** A CELEBRATION

# BMW

## A CELEBRATION

### Eric Dymock

ORION BOOKS / NEW YORK

Published in the United States by Orion Books, a division of Crown
Publishers, Inc., 201 East 50th Street, New York, New York 10022

Published in Great Britain by Pavilion Books Limited

Designed by Andrew Barron & Collis Clements Associates

ORION and colophon are trademarks of Crown Publishers, Inc.

Manufactured in West Germany

Library of Congress Cataloging-in-Publication Data

Dymock, Eric.
    BMW: a celebration/by Eric Dymock.
        p.      cm.
    1. BMW automobile—History. 2. BMW motorcycle—History.
    3. Bayerische Motoren Werke—History. I. Title.
    TL215.B25D86    1990
    629.222—dc20                                                90-6779
    ISBN 0–517-58047-0 (Crown)                                  CIP

10 9 8 7 6 5 4 3 2 1

First American Edition

## CONTENTS

Buying any car makes some sort of statement; buying a BMW says something profound. It displays a certain wealth; it shows taste and discrimination. It suggests a determination to enjoy driving, together with confidence in a seventy-five-year-old tradition of engineering and motor sport.

BMW has its origins in Germany's aircraft engines and motorcycles of the first quarter of the twentieth century. Its first V12 engine was not, as some might imagine, the one announced for the 750i in 1986, but a 47 litre, 600 horsepower aircraft engine made between 1926 and 1934 that won its spurs during long-distance flights in the Dornier Wal flying-boat.

BMW motorcycles played an important role in keeping the company afloat during hard times, and the flat-twin, shaft-drive machines became classics. In 1928 the purchase of the Eisenach Dixi works brought BMW into car manufacture, making Austin Sevens under licence, founding a dynasty that set bench-marks for saloon and touring cars for a generation of drivers which grew up in the 1930s. It was a generation that grew up in the shadow of war, heavily influenced by the design movements of the time, Art Deco, the Bauhaus architects, and the gratuitously curvy cars of Harley Earl.

They were years of design metaphors, such as the corporate identity programmes undertaken in Germany by the Allegemeine Electrizitäts Gesellschaft, or AEG, with its co-ordinated range of domestic and industrial appliances, and in England with the graphics, posters and architecture of London Transport. They

## INTRODUCTION

The divided windscreen of the BMW 328 folded flat to cut wind resistance for racing. Once the wing nuts at the side were loosened, the glass swivelled down flush with the bonnet top.

7

were the years of Le Corbusier's Villa Savoie in Poissy, and Raymond Loewy's Gestetner Duplicator.

BMW made its contribution to an era that saw Donald Wills Douglas's DC3 airliner start regular non-stop flights between New York and Chicago, Johnson Wax commission Frank Lloyd Wright to design its Head Office, and the German Standards Commission produce the proportions of A-sized paper. BMW added its name to the architects of the twentieth century, with the remarkable 328 of 1936, which

The BMW logo, evolved from the idea of a spinning aircraft propeller, was first used on a Munich Patent Office document, drawn up when the Rapp Motoren Werke became BMW in 1917.

changed the history, shape and specification of the sports car for ever.

The BMW story is not one of unbroken triumphs. Crises came and went, especially those connected with the two wars in which the firm was closely involved through the production of engines and vehicles. It is a story that includes the division of Germany, which left much of BMW on the wrong side of the fence. In 1945 the firm was dismembered, almost reappearing in Britain, when Bristol picked its brains. It is a story that includes the era of the

bubble car, the BMW Isetta on whose tiny wheels post-war Germany drove to its economic miracle. It is an industrial story, an engineering story, and a political story.

It is a story that includes the drama of motor racing, for BMW has consistently been involved in testing and trying its hand in the spotlight of international competition. It has pitted its wits against all comers, and achieved something only matched once in modern motor racing (by a Buick in 1966–67, as it happens) in providing the basis of a world championship-winning engine by using a production cylinder block.

BMW had financial predicaments, and moments of management uncertainty until the early 1960s, when the firm at last got into its stride, with a range of cars that provided the basis for its subsequent success.

Most of all it is a story of cars, from the almost comic Dixi to the classic 328, then to the bulbous, but well-made post-war V8s. They were not all great cars; the touring saloons of the pre-war years were notable more for their good solid worth than speed or *haute couture*.

The reputation of BMWs for speed and handling was forged in the 1970s, with the superbly smooth six-cylinder engines that became such a hallmark of BMW engineering. They enhanced the cars, and established them among the most respected in the world, making them not simply a well-made and sophisticated mode of transport, but cars to which people in all parts of the world would want to aspire.

*BMW: A Celebration* reflects this.

BMW originated in the aircraft industry in Munich, Bavaria, and the car industry in Eisenach, in the old province of Thuringia. From Bavaria comes the company title, the Bayerische Motoren Werke, Bavarian Motor Works, and that was essentially what it was to begin with – an engine works. BMW started before the First World War by making aero engines, then motorcycle engines, then motorcycles.

It did not get into cars until 1928, when it took over the Dixi company in Eisenach, where Martin Luther translated the Bible, and Johann Sebastian Bach was born. Dixi had been going since 1896, when it was set up by Heinrich Erhardt to make first Wartburg, then Dixi cars. Following the take-over, all BMW cars and many of the motorcycles were made here, throughout the years leading up to the Second World War.

So it was something of a historical accident that the car-making side of the business was in Eisenach at all, yet here it remained during the classic years of the 328s, which meant so much to BMW's reputation. A large range of BMW touring cars was also made in Eisenach, not all as fast nor as sporty as the 328, but they gained a reputation for good engineering, and a certain dash and flair, and established BMW in the developing European middle-class market.

Bavaria became once again the home of BMW cars in 1945, when BMW rebuilt on its traditional site to the north of the state capital, Munich, the self-styled Beer Capital of the world, where Mozart wrote *Idomeneo* and where Neville Chamberlain came to conclude

# THE

# FAMILY

# TREE

An early BMW 328 with un-drilled disc wheels. The two bonnet straps were standard equipment. The small lights under the headlights are a later, practical addition.

11

a peace agreement with Hitler in 1938, but made only history.

The largest state in the Federal Republic, Bavaria lies in the south-east, sharing borders with East Germany, Czechoslovakia and Austria. It is an independent place, with mountains, lakes, forests and farms, medieval towns and Baroque churches as well as industrial Munich. Here, where the Wittelsbachs ruled from 1180 till 1918, first over a duchy then a kingdom, BMW made its headquarters.

The modern headquarters BMW built in 1971, the famous 'four-cylinder' office block, the Hochhaus, that has come to be a Munich landmark, together with its accompanying museum, is on the site of the old flying field where the story begins. Here, on 15 March 1911, Gustav Otto, son of engine pioneer Nikolaus August Otto (of the four-stroke Otto cycle, patented in 1877), created the Gustav Otto Flugmaschinenfabrik (aircraft factory) München, at the eastern end of the Oberwiesenfeld airfield, on Lerchenauer Strasse.

By 1913, a merger was planned with the Karl Rapp Motorenwerke München GmbH, a small aero-engine workshop located at Schleissheimer Strasse 288, in nearby Milbertshofen. Together, Otto and Rapp created the grandly titled Flugwerke Deutschland (German Aircraft Factory) GmbH, first as the Bayerische Flugzeugwerke (Bavarian Aircraft Factory) AG on 7 March 1916, then the Bayerische Motoren-Werke (Bavarian Motor Works) GmbH on 21 July 1917.

Karl Friedrich Rapp, a former designer with the Daimler Motoren-Gesellschaft,

and a financier named Julius Auspitzer had been hoping for rich government and commercial contracts through a 90 horsepower, four-cylinder engine that Rapp had drawn up.

Optimistically installed in a spidery biplane, it was entered in a competition set up by the Kaiser in 1912, aimed at encouraging the new science of aviation, but the aircraft did not come up to expectations. It never even reached the final of the contest. Rapp's enthusiasm for setting himself up as an aero-engine manufacturer seemed to take little account of the fledgeling state of the German aircraft industry.

Not enough aeroplanes were being built to supply him with a market. Yet within two years of his failure in the Kaiserpreis, events in Europe put his business on a more secure footing. A nineteen-year-old Bosnian nationalist fired the starting pistol for the Great War, by assassinating Archduke Franz Ferdinand in his big Graf und Stift touring car.

Within months, the world was desperately buying aero engines – any aero engines. The Prussian War Ministry asked Rapp for twenty-five, regardless of the fact that they were not very good engines, and vibrated badly. Austria-Hungary wanted some too, and so did the Reichs Marine Authority. Rapp happily took on more workers. By the end of 1914, he had sixty-five, and began expanding the firm to take advantage of the flood of new orders.

He needed money; his partner Auspitzer helped out, and the firm was re-capitalized on 31 March 1915 to the tune of 175,000 Marks on condition that two of Auspitzer's sons-in-law could

Decorated for the visit of King Ludwig of Bavaria in 1915, the administration offices of the Rapp Motorenwerke.

Austrian Marines in the Rapp Motorenwerke assembling aircraft engines in 1917. On the left, Porsche-designed Austro-Daimler V-8s, on the right Rapp's upright straight-six.

join in. The firm acquired Erich Laeisz, of a Hamburg shipping family, and Max Wiedmann, among whose contacts was a wealthy financier in Vienna.

This was Camillo Castiglioni, who was born in Trieste when it was still part of the Austro-Hungarian Empire, and took up Italian citizenship after the war. At the height of his career he presided over a formidable empire of banking and industrial interests in Germany, Austria and the Balkans, but he always had an eye for the main chance, in the technical progress of the car and aircraft industries.

Castiglioni had a flair for publicity fitting his other role of press baron, and travelled in a personal monogrammed railway coach. He was a patron of the impresario Max Reinhardt in his early years, helped organize the first Salzburg Music Festivals, and contributed to the construction of the Salzburg Mozarteum, one of Europe's most distinguished musical foundations.

Following the Second World War, Castiglioni took President Tito of Yugoslavia before the Italian courts for unpaid commission on a $40 million loan negotiated with the Export-Import Bank of Washington. He won the case, and Yugoslav Government property in Italy was sequestered to pay him off, but before he could enjoy the recovery in his fortunes, he died in Rome at the age of seventy-six. A keen art collector, he had accumulated a collection which was worth several million dollars at the time of his death in 1957.

As head of the Vienna Bank Association in 1915, the colourful Castiglioni had already made some shrewd investments in cars and aero engines with Austro-Daimler, and would play a continuing role in the fortunes of BMW.

By the time of the 1915 re-capitalization, Flugwerke Deutschland had 370 employees, yet prosperity still proved to be elusive, even with help from the Bayerische Vereinsbank. The engines still vibrated, and sales suffered as smoother-running rivals came on to the market, and not for the last time in the history of BMW and its forebears, financial difficulties loomed large. The only real hope for rescue lay in Wiedmann's enigmatic friend, the Austro-Hungarian commerce commissioner, Castiglioni.

Not only had Castiglioni access to lots of money but, as a result of his large holdings in Austro-Daimler, he was able to influence the licensing arrangements for a new V12 engine, designed under its Technical Director, Ferdinand Porsche. He knew of an order for 225 engines which Austro-Daimler was unable to meet, so he was already on the look-out for a company which could make them to Austro-Daimler's satisfaction, and his own personal profit.

He found it in Flugwerke Deutschland, shortly to be renamed Bayerische Flugzeugwerke AG. The Austrian authorities were reluctant at first to allow manufacture of the engine in Germany, so made it a condition that a resident Austrian engineer should oversee the work. The task fell to a young air force officer, Franz-Josef Popp, a graduate of the Technische Hochschule in Brünn, who had encouraged Porsche to make a prototype of the V12 at Austro-Daimler, and now wanted to see it through to production.

Before the war Popp had been an electrical engineer with AEG. At the outbreak of war he took up his post in military procurement, as an expert in aviation. A key figure in lobbying the authorities, it was Popp whom Castiglioni had to thank for not only

initiating the design of the engine, but persuading the Austrian Government to sanction production in Germany.

Technical Director Porsche regarded Castiglioni's manoeuvrings with deep suspicion, and was less than pleased when he discovered that his engine was to be produced elsewhere. The deal went ahead just the same, Rapp agreed to make it, and the wily Castiglioni collected a commission of 2.5 million Marks and more shares in Austro-Daimler. Wiedmann and Rapp collected a down-payment of 7 million Marks to set up production, and young Lieutenant Popp was sent to the small workshop in the Schleissheimer Strasse to supervise construction on behalf of the Austrian Government.

Castiglioni's commission more than covered a small investment he had made in Rapp and Wiedmann's firm so he was able to enjoy his profits on a continuing basis. On 13 August 1918, the firm was again restructured as the Bayerische Motoren-Werke AG, with a further investment from Castiglioni. There was now a total of 3,400 employees, working in shifts to meet the demand.

The V12 went into production, but it was soon replaced by another engine that would become an important product to the newly established BMW. During Rapp's spell at the Daimler works in the Stuttgart suburb of Cannstatt, he came to know a young Swabian engineer, Max Friz. Rapp had left to set up on his own, but Friz remained in the design office under Gottlieb Daimler's son, Paul. Generally, the younger Daimler got on well with Friz, but when he refused him promotion in 1916, Friz made up his mind to leave. He got in

Camillo Castiglioni, a key figure in the early development of BMW, effectively controlled the Austrian aircraft industry at the outbreak of the First World War. By 1940 he was being accused of profiteering and exploitation.

High quality aluminium castings were an important feature of BMW engines from the early days. A prospectus of 1919.

touch with Rapp, but, to his intense disappointment, was received with scant enthusiasm.

Fortunately Franz-Josef Popp and Max Wiedmann were able to over-rule the hard-pressed Rapp. Friz had already gained something of a reputation in the aero-engine business, but more important than that at a critical stage of the war, he came with the plans for a high-altitude power unit designed at his former employer's.

Not only did Friz bring with him the 19 litre, water-cooled six-cylinder engine that was to become the famous BMW IIIa, but having worked on the 1914 Mercedes Grand Prix engine, he was also able to help Rapp solve some of the technical and production problems with which he was continually beset.

The IIIa was such an immediate success that it became BMW's turn to license its manufacture. The first thousand production engines were built by Opel, while a new plant at Oberwiesenfeld was constructed to make them for the embattled German Air Force. The extensive works put up in 1917–18 at Moosacher Strasse made engines for aircraft such as the most successful German fighter of the war, the Fokker D VII, production versions of which were delivered in the spring of 1918. By that autumn, over forty fighter units were equipped with D VIIs.

Yet for Rapp, the euphoria was short-lived. The strain of creating the company and sustaining it was too much for him. He felt he had failed as an engineer through having to manufacture engines designed by somebody else, so he resigned as Technical Director, to be replaced by

Popp, now firmly identified with the joint company.

Friz improved the IIIa's high-altitude performance, and called it the BMW IV, but it came too late to change the course of the war, and only seventy of the two thousand ordered were ever delivered. By then the company was close to liquidation, and by 19 August 1918 it was all over. The old facilities at Schleissheimer Strasse were kept for a while as design offices and experimental workshops, but had to be sold off, as the Treaty of Versailles forbade the construction of aircraft in Germany. As the Treaty began to take effect, the entire BMW enterprise had to face up to a complete reorganization.

In the hiatus that followed, the Bayerische Motoren-Werke had to take what work it could get. Otto went off to make Flottweg motorcycles in 1921, and BMW, or such Bavarian motor works as remained, gratefully received an order for railway brakes from Knorr-Bremse AG. The former Flugzeugwerke gladly built tool storage cabinets and office furniture. Any hope of making aero engines for civilian use, at least in the short term, disappeared when the order was given for the destruction of the workshop machinery, and all the components and parts already manufactured. Existing engines were taken as war reparations and used all over the world, which had its compensations in spreading their reputation well beyond the frontiers of Germany.

The problems of readjustment after the war were not confined to Germany, and many firms in Britain and elsewhere, swollen for war production, were left with useless excess capacity.

Gustav Otto, not yet thirty, and already a pilot, flying instructor, aircraft constructor, and businessman.

There was a sudden proliferation of car manufacturing throughout Europe, in the expectation that the post-war world would want wheels in large numbers for the homecoming millions. In the event, the millions could not afford many cars, and scores of hopeful car-makers went to the wall in the early 1920s.

BMW was less ambitious. It saw its future in engines of all kinds – engines for power generation, for ships, for motorcycles, tractors, vehicles of all kinds. Friz identified possibilities in the motorcycle market, but the order for ten thousand brakes for the Bavarian railways which came through Popp's contacts with the omniscient Castiglioni was too important to turn down. And while the *manufacture* of aero engines was forbidden, Popp managed to keep his engineers busy with some illicit development work on the high-altitude unit, with which the test-pilot Zeno Diemer was to set records.

The contract for the railway brakes nearly led BMW into partnership with Knorr-Bremse AG of Berlin, the licensor. Anxious to recoup losses he had made following the German collapse, Castiglioni sold out his part of BMW to Knorr-Bremse, which wanted to acquire workshop capacity. But becoming a subsidiary was not part of Popp's plans, and he turned Knorr down. This was by no means the end of Castiglioni's involvement with BMW.

Cars seemed a likely market to Popp – as they did to the twenty-nine other factories in Germany that were determined to make them. Everyone was convinced he had the key to prosperity, and once again Castiglioni came up with a scheme that looked as though it would work. He had

discovered, through his old contacts at Austro-Daimler, that Ferdinand Porsche was working on a small car. Post-war Germany, its borders still more or less intact, would be a better place to sell it than within the redrawn boundaries of post-war Austria. Since Austria was now so much smaller, reasoned the Vienna bank commissioner, it would have fewer potential customers than it did before.

Dr Porsche had been designing the Sascha, following encouragement from Count Alexander (Sascha) Kolowrat, who wanted to develop it into a sports car. It had a four-cylinder, 1100cc overhead camshaft engine, giving between 40 and 50 horsepower, and a prototype made by Austro-Daimler did nearly 90mph in 1922. Popp and Friz were certainly interested. Alas, the Sascha is remembered chiefly as the car which launched the driving career of Alfred Naubauer, one of the most successful team managers in the history of motor racing, rather than for its commercial success. Porsche once again discovered Castiglioni's plans to manufacture one of his designs elsewhere, and this time put a stop to them. BMW had to wait a further five years before it could think again about putting the blue and white roundel on the front of a car.

The Sascha went on to score racing successes, notably in the Targa Florio, but pursuit of glory on the racetrack was to be Porsche's downfall. The directors of Austro-Daimler wanted sales more than a racy reputation, they fell out with their Technical Director, and in 1923 he resigned and went to Daimler in Stuttgart.

In the event it was just as well that BMW

The car that eluded BMW. The victorious Austro-Daimler Sascha team in the 1922 Targa Florio. Max Friz and Franz-Josef Popp tried to buy the Porsche design.

*Overleaf*: the ignition/mixture control on the steering wheel of a 3/18 of 1932, still bearing traces of Austin Seven ancestry.

kept out of car manufacturing for the time being. The market was still small; only 25,000 new cars were sold in Germany in 1923, many of them cheap imports from America, and a newcomer to the industry would have found it impossible to make headway. It was hard enough for the established manufacturers. Some even went so far as to copy American designs, but they were unable to compete on price with imports from the United States.

Castiglioni was not finished yet, however. In 1922 he bought back from Knorr-Bremse all the licence rights for the brakes BMW had been making for 75 million Reichsmarks, a shrewd deal under which he paid for them in US dollars. When he came to put his cash into BMW, however, it was in rather less worthy German currency. Meanwhile Johann Vielmetter of Knorr was left with the former BMW plant in Moosacher Strasse, only completed in the closing months of the war. He could not even do what he pleased with it, for a clause in the sale forbade him to use the word *motoren* in the title of any company he might establish there.

Moosacher Strasse became the home of the Suddeutsche Bremsen AG, many of whose best employees, Vielmetter found, began defecting to BMW in the Lerchenauer Strasse to do something more interesting than making brakes.

BMW was obliged to fulfil the brakes order, yet it continued to regard itself as an engine-making company, and since it was forbidden to make aero engines, something else had to be found. Taking the six-cylinder overhead cam IIIa as a basis, Friz developed a four-cylinder industrial engine, which was pressed into service for ships, lorries, buses,

tractors of a sort, and stationary power plants.

The adaptation and development of an outstanding basic design, already a well-established practice at Eisenach, also took root under Friz's regime at BMW.

These were tough times, and BMW built a tough engine for them. Some of the plans had to be concealed behind heating ducts, to escape detection by the Allied Control Commission. Yet the engine was made, a large 8 litre affair which was unusual in having a single overhead camshaft, common enough in racing or high-performance engines, but less so on a 540kg (1,190lb) power unit to be used in trucks or on farms. Some remained in service for many years, and there were still enquiries for spares well into the 1950s.

In 1921, searching for alternative products to keep the business going, Friz designed a horizontally opposed, air-cooled twin-cylinder engine of 500cc. Known as the M2B15, and called a boxer-motor because the pistons worked in opposite directions, with their connecting-rods flailing like boxers' arms, the Bayern-Kleinmotor (Bavarian small engine), as it came to be known, developed 6 horsepower.

Aero engines remained the principal product of BMW for most of the 1920s, yet the management stuck to a three-pronged policy which turned out to be important for the continued success of the enterprise. When one side of the business was in decline, the others kept it going. Aero engines represented the profit centre of the 1920s, backed up by the motorcycles. By the early 1930s, cars were coming in – just in time, as it

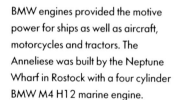

BMW engines provided the motive power for ships as well as aircraft, motorcycles and tractors. The Anneliese was built by the Neptune Wharf in Rostock with a four cylinder BMW M4 H12 marine engine.

Sea-going BMW, the M4 H12 engine was a marine version of BMW's stationary engine used as an industrial and agricultural power plant. Some survivors were working well into the 1950s.

Visiting dignitaries at Eisenach. Henrich Erhardt with the nobility and gentry. The founder of the Fahrzeugfabrik Eisenach (centre) with the Grand Ducal family of Sachsen-Weimer-Eisenach and its entourage trying out some early Wartburgs.

happened, to save the company from the decline in aero engines.

On 5 May 1922, the prohibition on aero engines was lifted, and by the end of 1923 BMW was turning out twenty-five a month. Motorcycle production was also under way, and despite the rebuff from Dr Porsche, the management had not altogether stopped thinking about cars. Mauser, a famous name in weapons, had made some cars with the little M2B15 engine, and Friz and Popp had experimented with it, in a Czechoslovak Tatra with front wheel drive, but without much distinction.

The management was also involved with Dipl.-Ing. Wunibald Kamm, a professor at the Stuttgart Technical University, a noted aerodynamicist and brilliant theoretician. He had persuaded the Swabian Steel Works to sponsor an all-aluminium, unit-construction car with a water-cooled, twin-cylinder boxer engine driving the

front wheels, and BMW got the job of making the three prototypes.

They were advanced cars for their day. This was the era of the Lancia Lambda, and the front wheels were independently suspended with oleo coil-sprung struts. Unfortunately, Professor Kamm's technology was ahead of its time. The complexities of his design would have been beyond a major car constructor with years of experience, far less an upstart such as BMW.

Friz turned down the idea of manufacturing the car, on the grounds of cost, but Kamm's work was not entirely in vain. His prescience must have made an impression, because he continued working for BMW on a consultancy basis until 1940.

Meanwhile, in Eisenach, the Dixi-Werke had evolved into a vehicle factory rather than simply a car factory. As befitted a man who made his fortune manufacturing artillery, rapid-firing cannon, armour plate and machine tools, Heinrich Erhardt was not going to put all his eggs in the car-making basket. Eisenach made gun carriages, military vehicles, ambulances, field-kitchens and bicycles (notably mountain bicycles with a novel shaft drive), taking eight years even to settle on petrol engines as a source of motive power. The Wartburg Electric was the mainstay of production until Erhardt negotiated a licence to build cars based on the French Decauville in September 1898.

At the end of the nineteenth century, buying somebody else's design was the only means a firm had if it wanted to make cars at all. It was difficult for anyone to draw up his own, so long as an intimate knowledge of the technique was confined to a small number of inventors and developers. Licensing was not always satisfactory. In Britain, the rascally Harry Lawson used patents and licensing agreements to create a car manufacturing monopoly, devising the British Motor Syndicate in 1895, and buying every patent and licence he could lay his hands on. He leased or sold them to nominees, and tried to exact a royalty on every car made or imported.

Lawson's schemes were for the most part either fraudulent or farcical, but elsewhere in the history of the motor industry, licences played an important role. They were crucial to BMW car manufacture on at least two occasions, and licensing arrangements provided the firm with one of the most successful aero engines it ever made.

The Decauville that Eisenach agreed to

build was a very satisfactory design of the time, and the Société Decauville was well established. It started making cars in 1898 as a sideline, and turned out a neat, tubular-framed voiturette. Its rear-mounted, twin-cylinder, 3½ litre air-cooled engine was really two De Dion cylinders on a common crankcase. The rear axle was unsprung, but the Decauville was a pioneer in independent front suspension.

There is no evidence to support the story that it was disappointment with his Decauville which inspired young Henry Royce to design his first car. On the contrary, despite the crudeness of its exposed gearing, the Decauville was reliable, though noisy, and was in production at Eisenach by the end of 1898, taking the name Wartburg from the local castle.

An Eisenach tradition subsequently handed on to BMW was an evolutionary approach to design. Radical new models were rarely to be BMW's habit, and both cars and motorcycles were modified stage by stage. They were changed when change was necessary rather than changed for change's sake. The evolution of the Decauville by Eisenach was a case in point.

Erhardt hired a brilliant young engineer, Arthur Rebling, to develop it. He was twenty-five when he came to Eisenach, with a degree from the Karlsruhe Technical University and three years' experience at the Chicago Western Wheel Works. Rebling first developed the car into Eisenach's own 5 horsepower, water-cooled version, then in 1902 made another of 8.5 horsepower. By 1899 it was called a Wartburg, and had acquired proper

BMW advertising reflected the diversity of the company's products after aero-engine construction was forbidden by the Treaty of Versailles.

rear springs, and a portable garage was offered as an incentive to buy one.

Alas, it was not enough. Cars were not good earners, and as bicycle and military sales went into decline, Erhardt pulled out, taking the Decauville licence with him.

The Fahrzeugfabrik Eisenach was left with its debts, and without its principal product, in charge of another engineer, Willy Seck. There was nothing for it, but to create its own home-grown design, and make it work.

Seck created the Dixi. The name was adopted from the Latin for 'I have spoken', and it claimed to be the last word in cars. It established another tradition that BMW followed in the years to come. It was produced in relatively small numbers, and sold at a premium price.

The expensive quality car business still lay in the future, however. By the mid-1920s, the German market had had enough of US-style saloons. Opel was still the market leader, but in decline and losing money through misjudging the market, and trying to sell big six-cylinder cars. General Motors was waiting in the wings to take it over.

Fritz von Opel had seen the way things were going, though. In 1924 he bought a Citroën 5CV, a basic economy car, and had it carefully copied and put into production. The 4/12 horsepower model that became known as the Laufrosch (tree-frog) was made on a moving assembly line after the Ford pattern, and at 4,000 Reichsmarks the orders poured in.

Unfortunately, the tree-frog proved a

little too close to the original Citroën; the French company sued, and Opel was forced to stop making it. The firm changed it in 1927, by which time General Motors was in charge, and when it reappeared at 2,700 Reichsmarks it was such a success that 42,771 were made in 1928 alone.

The lesson was not lost on Dixi, but while the future clearly lay in small cars, Eisenach did not have one. What it did have, however, was an owner who knew how to get one.

Jakob Schapiro was born in Odessa on the Black Sea in 1885. He appeared in Vienna during the war, then moved to Berlin, becoming something of an entrepreneur whose business empire included garages, a taxi company, a coachwork company, and holdings in car-makers NSU, in Heilbronn, and Cyklon, of Mylau in Saxony. Schapiro also had a major interest in Benz, at Mannheim, and the Daimler Motoren Gesellschaft of Stuttgart. And when Benz and Daimler came together in 1926, sitting on the board of the merged Daimler-Benz Company was none other than Franz-Josef Popp, General Director of BMW.

Daimler-Benz resisted Schapiro's entreaties for business on behalf of his Schebera coachbuilding firm, so he turned to another of his enterprises, the Gothaer Waggonfabrik, which built railway cars, and which had merged with the Eisenach Dixi factory in 1921. What Schapiro needed for his industrial realm was liquidity, and merging Gothaer-Eisenach with his ailing Cyklon works enabled him to raise credit of 4 million Marks.

He also merged Schebera with NSU,

Downdraught carburettors feeding six hungry cylinders made the 328 a tall engine. Bonnet-top air intakes were a feature of later Bristol-engined racing cars. The OZ 80 (for Oktanzahl 80) on the cam covers means this is one of the much sought-after racing engines with high-compression pistons.

and by 1927 was running the second-largest motor industry group in Germany after Daimler-Benz. But it was a badly managed enterprise, and, with the crisis of 1929 looming, the banks were becoming restive. Eisenach's sales were slipping, a small car was needed, and there was no time to design and develop one before the banks foreclosed.

Schapiro eyed the Austin Seven, which was being sold in Germany by Koch und Weichsel of Berlin. He was not the first to spot the opportunity; Bernhard Stoewer of Stettin had been talking to Austin, but withdrew, leaving Schapiro to negotiate a licensing agreement to build two thousand cars a year, using German raw materials, to be sold in Germany and Eastern Europe.

Secretly, Schapiro planned to cheat, and make three hundred cars a week, an annual total of 12,500. The first fifty cars were assembled from British components in September 1927, and within two months a German-made version was on sale. A year later, Eisenach had made nine thousand examples of the Dixi 3/15. Success in the already forbidding financial climate of 1928 seemed likely, but Dixi owed more than 5 million Marks to the banks, and Schapiro had had to borrow 6 million more in order to get the car into production.

The banks, however, believed the old motor industry maxim that small cars would only make small profits, and Schapiro's empire came close to collapse. He had to separate Cyklon from Eisenach and try to foist it on an unhappy NSU, which, in the end, he was forced to sell off to Fiat. The banks were closing in, and he was more than

glad when his fellow Daimler-Benz board member, Franz-Josef Popp, revealed that BMW was interested in buying Eisenach.

The Dixi 3/15 was exactly what Popp had been looking for. The ever-present Castiglioni turned up as negotiator and agreed that BMW ought to build a car, but not one that would compete with Daimler-Benz, in which he, Popp, Dr Emil Georg von Stauss of the Deutsche Bank, and Schapiro all had an interest. In 1928 Schapiro owned 18.3 per cent of Daimler-Benz, the bank 10 per cent, and Castiglioni 3.4 per cent, so there could be no question of BMW moving into the D-B market.

Eisenach was sold to BMW in September 1928 for 15 million Marks. Schapiro's fortunes now took a turn for the worse; he lost his seat on the Daimler-Benz board, and by 1931 his career as a motor industry mogul was at an end.

Castiglioni's financial empire suffered a number of setbacks too, until in 1926 he was forced to transfer his activities to Switzerland and Italy, setting up a private bank in Milan. But by then he too had surrendered his position in the world of industry and commerce, for the time being at least.

As for Franz-Josef Popp, after fending off Knorr-Bremse he became General Director of BMW, a position he held for the next twenty years. In 1929 Castiglioni's shareholding was taken over by the Deutsche Bank, Popp negotiated an aero-engine contract with Pratt and Whitney, and the end of the beginning of BMW was within sight.

This was the scene when BMW, now

BMW takes over. Eisenach-made Austin Sevens, now officially BMW Dixis, are taken from the factory. The cars are DA2 models, which dates the photograph around July 1929. The lorries are 4-ton Dixis dating back to 1921.

well established in the aero-engine and motorcycle fields, acquired Eisenach and its Austin Seven lookalike.

The Dixi-Werke had been a progressive company, making good cars in a difficult market. Like BMW in Munich, it had commissioned from Paul Jaray an aerodynamic study of a slippery-looking saloon. In 1924, Gläser of Dresden built the car, known as the G.1, on a Dixi 6/24 chassis, with a deeply curved windscreen, built-in headlights, and a pointed tail. It was a profound design that anticipated many aerodynamic trends by fully twenty years, but Dixi never built it, preferring the rather staid cars to which its customers had grown accustomed.

Aerodynamics were just about the last thing in Herbert Austin's mind when he planned, in secret, a car with the ground area of a motorcycle and sidecar, and seats for four. Austin set aside the billiard room of his home at Lickey Grange, Bromsgrove, south-west of Birmingham, close to the heart of the British motor industry, for a young draughtsman to draw up a car that would revolutionize design in much the same way as the Mini, nearly forty years later.

The keynote of the Baby Austin was simplicity; it was designed for the post-war motoring boom expected in Britain no less than Germany, and despite a derisive reception by the press, scored an immediate success when it was announced in 1922.

Ironically, in view of the later connection with BMW, Herbert Austin, later Lord Austin, wanted to use a flat-twin engine, but he was unable to make a prototype run smoothly

enough, and since the Seven had to defeat the vogue-ish cyclecars, it had to be a proper car in miniature, with all the features of its full-sized adversaries. Accordingly, he made a four-cylinder, 747cc, side-valve engine with a two-bearing crankshaft, of 13 horsepower.

Its performance was modest, acceleration leisurely, and luxuries such as an electric starter, coil ignition, and a four-speed gearbox had to wait until later versions. It did have four-wheel brakes – the pedal worked the rear ones and the handbrake operated those at the front. A contemporary road-test complained that it took 56 feet to accomplish a stop from 30mph.

Yet it was such a success, and export markets so flourished, that it was built in France as the Rosengart, in the United States as the Bantam, and was even copied illegally by Datsun in Japan. Before Eisenach started making it in Germany, the Berlin importer had sold several thousand Austin Sevens.

The basis of the Seven was a simple A-shaped chassis frame with the radiator and the engine at the apex of the 'A', and quarter-elliptic leaf-springs jutting from the stub ends of the main side-members, supporting the back axle. A single, rather spindly transverse leaf-spring at the front, and no means of steadying the front or rear axles meant that handling was not the Seven's strongest feature. But since attaining the top speed of about 50mph occupied something over half a minute, it was a relatively safe car by the standards of the 1920s.

*Top:* the crest used on Eisenach letterheads and catalogues between 1903 and 1914. *Middle:* the centaur cypher on commercial vehicle advertising 1914–28. *Bottom:* the Dixi radiator emblem and dealer sign between 1923 and the BMW takeover in 1928.

The eve of the Great Depression was not the best time to start making cars, but in the circumstances an economy car was clearly appropriate. Besides, BMW's motorcycle business was doing sufficiently well to allow a risk to be taken on four-wheelers. Throughout the years of economic hardship, low running costs were critical, so motorcycles were a good starting-point. The Austin Seven was also the logical car to take over, since it had been conceived as a car to which a motorcycle owner would be happy to graduate.

Germany was settling down to a period of relative calm; the reform of the monetary system had been a success, the Treaty of Locarno signed, and Allied troops began to leave the Rhineland. The world had not yet got over the monetary and business upheaval of the First World War, however, and the financial climate remained harsh. In April 1929, BMW offered cars and motorcycles on a form of hire purchase. A DA 2, the first true BMW/Austin, could be paid off in twenty-four instalments of 107 Reichsmarks. Then, within a year of BMW signing the contract to take over Eisenach, the Wall Street Crash precipitated the great depression. The world economy, built up so painfully thoughout the 1920s, was once again plunging into crisis.

The time of the small car was clearly at hand, yet no sooner had BMW got its hand on the plain, basic, no-frills little Austin, than it began to change it. By July 1929, the car had a new radiator shape and bigger doors, and the open two-seater had lost its running boards and gained proper side-curtains, to keep out the Bavarian winter.

## THE

## FIRST

## BMW

## CARS

Most BMW 315 models were equipped with disc, not wire wheels as in this example. The spats over the rear wheels were vulnerable to damage and often removed by owners.

BMW developed a closed steel saloon, with the body built by Ambi-Budd in Berlin, and the name was changed. The first batch of a hundred Dixi-Sevens had been made from imported components. The first locally-made ones, DA 1 (Deutsche Ausführung, German Version No. 1), were made with BMW badges from the beginning of 1929, and from July 1929 they became the DA 2, the first production car to embody BMW engineering.

The DA 2 also had proper four-wheel brakes; Herbert Austin's primitive system clearly offended Friz's engineering principles, and the car was made to grow up in other ways. It began to look less spidery and justify the advertising slogan 'Larger inside than it is outside'. The sliding windows were changed to winding ones, and the letter-box sized rear window was enlarged. The name was duly changed to the 3/15, and between July 1929 and March 1931 BMW sold 12,468 of them, coming second in the German sales league behind Opel. The Dixi's rivals, the 750cc Hanomag and the two-stroke DKW were left well behind.

It was just as well that the cars and motorcycles were selling in satisfactory numbers, because the aviation side of the business was beginning to suffer from the depression. The BMW see-saw principle under which car, bike and aero-engine divisions compensated for one another in bad times had to come into play, as government orders dried up, because civil aviation had not taken off with the vigour wartime ex-aviators had expected.

Charles Lindbergh's historic Atlantic flight in 1927 may have caught the public imagination, but most of them

Winning in the 1932 Baden-Baden *Schönheitswettbewerb* Concours, a BMW 3/20. The 3 represented taxation horsepower, the 20 the maximum engine horsepower. Daimler-Benz at Sindelfingen made the body for this model.

considered flying much as a later generation would think of space flight – thrilling, but strictly for the daring and well-trained aviator. Lay-offs in the car industry reduced its workforce by a third, and BMW still had to deal with the debts it had taken over with Eisenach.

Not all of the alterations to Lord Austin's baby car were successful. The DA 4, introduced at the Berlin Motor Show in 1931, had a body 20cm longer, still more changes to the radiator, and rather weighty-looking pressed steel wheels. Unfortunately it suffered from a swing-axle front suspension which rendered the already uncertain handling more than a little precarious.

More changes nevertheless went ahead. Friz had been working on a front wheel drive twin-cylinder two-stroke, to try and keep up with the acceleration of the DKW. It failed to provide the expected turn of speed, so he persevered with the car he had, rather than inventing anything radical. It established the safe, careful tradition for BMW, of well-bred rather than sensationally different cars, and made the Dixi, apart from the shaky swing-axle front springing, faster, roomier and easier to sell.

Yet Friz still wanted BMW to develop its own car, and by 1 March 1932 the firm felt confident enough to cancel the licensing agreement with Austin, and develop the BMW 3/20. The engine came in for a fundamental change, with roller main bearings and overhead valves. The internal model code became AM 1 (for Auto München No. 1), and the box-frame chassis was replaced by a central spine, supporting a plumper, heavier, but solidly finished body made by Daimler-Benz AG at Sindelfingen.

Gustav Otto with an Argus aero engine.

The trouble was that while direction and engine engineering were concentrated in Munich, chassis engineering stayed at Eisenach, where it remained rooted in the style and standards of the past. The backbone chassis frame was radical enough; Dr Porsche was toying with one for the V3, the prototype Volkswagen which he was building in the garage of his villa in Stuttgart, before it evolved into a platform-style underframe.

Dr Porsche kept swing-axle suspension for the rear of the VW, so Eisenach was not completely out of step with contemporary thinking. It was more a case of not keeping ahead, and while Porsche adopted trailing arms for the VW's front suspension, Eisenach kept the earlier swing-axle arrangement from the DA 4.

The novel swing-axle system at the rear had two transverse leaf-springs supporting the wheel hub-carriers. But the combination of swing-axles at both ends of the car meant that the wheels continuously followed graceful curving paths, with the tyres sometimes gripping the road with a flat footprint, and sometimes not. The weakness of swing-axles is that as the wheels spring up and down, they move in an arc, so they do not remain perpendicular to the road. As they tilt over, the shape of the patch gripping the road surface changes from oval to triangular, with the grip diminishing accordingly. The further they tilt, the less the grip, and as each tyre's contact patch constantly changes, so also does the grip of each wheel, with consequences that may be felt at the wheel of a BMW 3/20.

They are consequences that can also be felt at the wheel of an early-model

*Following pages:* The voluptuous 327. Made from 1937 to 1941, the 327 had the chassis and engine of the 326 and the shortened chassis of the 320. The headlights were sunk into the cowl, establishing the frontal aspect of BMWs for the best of two decades to come.

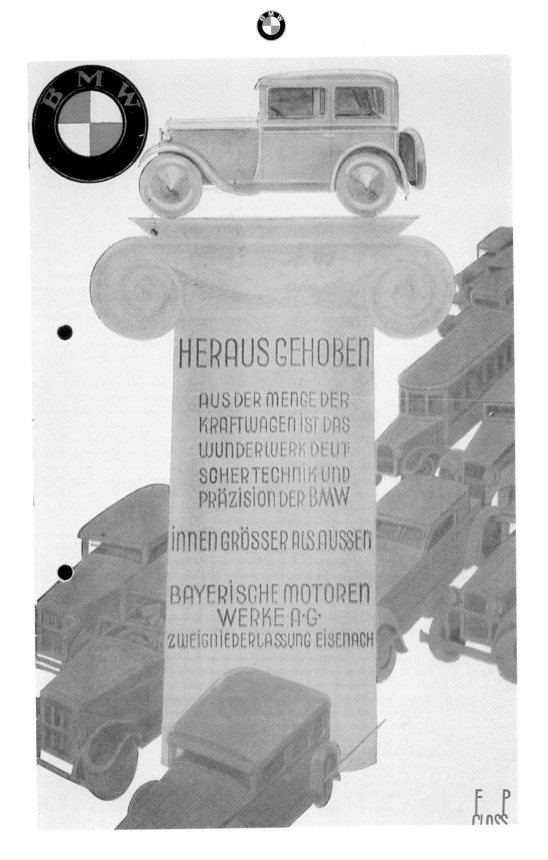

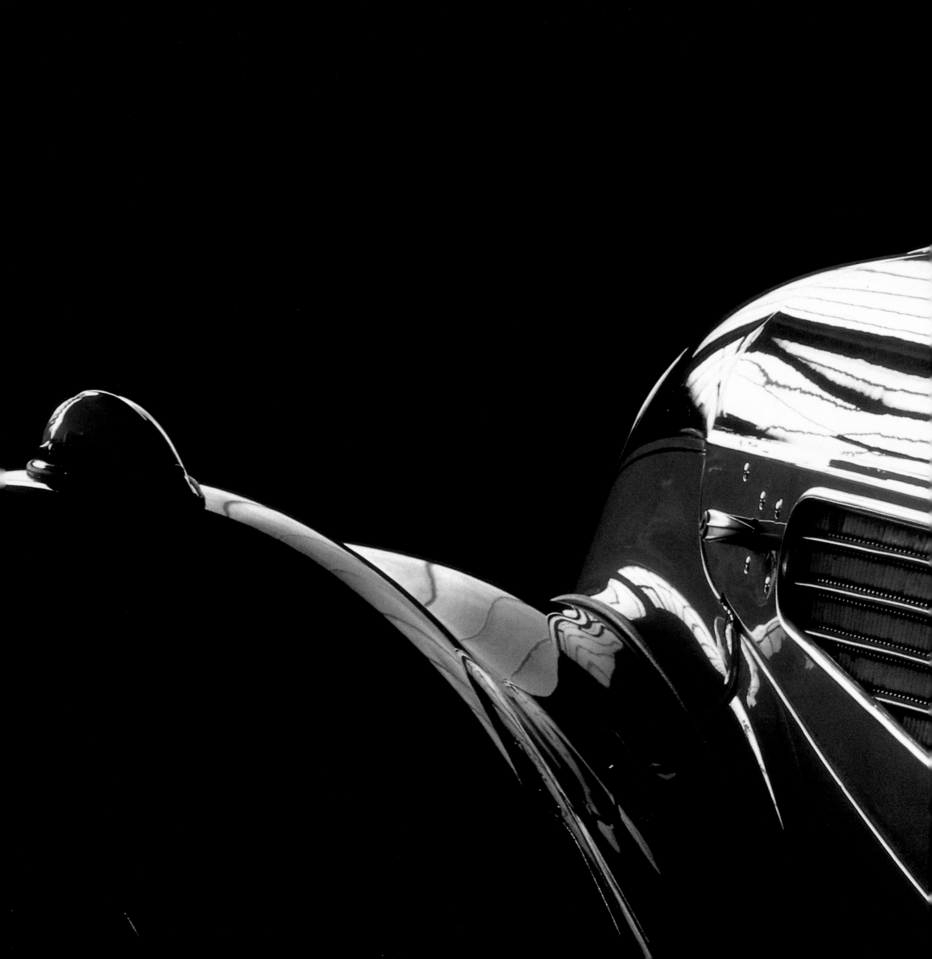

VW Beetle. The rear gets up on its swing-axles and dithers about, the rear tyres gripping with their shoulders as they bounce. With swing-axles at both ends, a 3/20 could only be twice as bad.

Imperfections of braking and handling apart, the 3/20 (the AM 4 by 1934), was a mature little car which, like the Seven in Britain, attracted specialist coachwork, giving it a touch of excitement as well as an extra turn of speed. There were even fashionable cabriolets from the likes of Reutter, of Stuttgart, and Ludwig Weiberger, of Munich.

So, the ingredients of the classic BMWs were gradually being put together: Eisenach set a fine tradition of high-quality construction, even if its chassis engineering took time to develop; Munich supplied the essential technical virility; while enterprising outsiders added a touch of glamour to a line of cars still essentially workman-like, economical and practical. The idea of BMWs as anything beyond primary transportation had not yet been floated, and it was only with the advent of the first six-cylinder engine that BMWs graduated from being mere conveyances to transports of delight.

The pedigree of modern BMWs can be traced back to the 303, the first 3-Series in effect, announced in June 1933. The bore and stroke dimensions of the 1.2 litre six-cylinder were the same as those of the AM 4 four-cylinder. The camshaft drive was by duplex chain, and with twin Solex carburettors it produced an impressive 30 horsepower. The foundations of later, greater BMWs were being laid.

Exports were important to Eisenach. A big Dixi 9/40 touring car poses in the Ukraine in this poster of 1927–29.

The first batch of bodies came from Daimler-Benz at Sindelfingen, later ones from Ambi-Budd in Berlin. Making bodies with steel pressings was still a relatively new business; the mainly wood-framed bodies of the 1920s had given way to assemblies put together from a number of metal parts stamped out on huge presses, and built by specialist press-shops.

The big American companies, Briggs, Budd, Fisher and Murray, now had European counterparts. In Britain, Pressed Steel had been launched by William Morris (later Lord Nuffield) in 1927. Budd patented a body-making system which pressed out the entire side of a car, in one piece. The sections were then welded together and the bodies painted before being sent off to the car manufacturer, now more of an assembler, who put in seats, carpets and wiring, and added the other components: engine, gearbox, axles and suspension.

Ambi-Budd was the German licensee of the Budd system, and besides BMW, built bodies for Adler, Audi, Ford, Hanomag, and the large luxury Horch, a Mercedes competitor. The body styles for the 303 included two-door saloons, cabriolets, and a portent of things to come, a stylish two-seat sports car.

In the event, the model was relatively short-lived. BMW was steadily evolving, and only 3,210 of the well-proportioned little 303s were ever made, the first production BMWs to feature the *nierenformig*, kidney-shaped radiator.

Eisenach had developed a stronger chassis frame made from 90mm tubular steel, with a rather safer transversely

Eisenach's 6/24 sports car was so successful that in 1924 the works commissioned Paul Jaray to design this streamliner. Rather tall and narrow, it nevertheless anticipated many design trends that were not seen again until the 1930s.

sprung front axle. More importantly, it discarded the uncertainties of the wobbly swing-axles at the rear, and reverted to a live one-piece axle on conventional leaf-springs which made up in security what it may have lacked in adventure. There was also the novelty of an unusually direct rack and pinion steering that distinguished the 303 as the best-handling BMW yet.

It was discontinued in April 1934, and replaced by two logically-titled cars, the 309, with a four-cylinder 0.9 litre engine, and the 315, a six-cylinder 1.5 litre, really the 303 with a longer piston stroke. Having given the model a number (in this case 3) followed by the engine size (0.9 litre and 1.5 – in later years 2.0 or 1.8), BMW had evolved a numbering system that would serve them well down the years. Inevitably, there were inconsistencies, but it provided a convenient means of identifying the cars from then on, and 3-Series, 5-series and 7-Series have become a useful shorthand in distinguishing one range of models from another.

The four-cylinder cars continued, but, conscious of the smoothness of the new sixes, BMW had another engineering trick up its sleeve. This was the *Schwebemotor*, or suspended engine, which was no more than rubber mountings for the fours at two points on the chassis.

The 309 properly replaced the former Dixi 3/20, and can be consigned to the ranks of BMWs that were worthy but hardly notable. The 315, however, did establish BMW as a manufacturer of cars with ambitions towards high performance. Its legacy to later models was the light, twin-tube frame, the transverse-leaf independent front suspension greatly refined and civilized, the pushrod overhead-valve engine, with four main bearings, and the four-speed synchromesh transmission.

The basic 34 horsepower, twin-carburettor version was not specially swift and could manage only about 62mph. Speed was not yet a priority, which was perhaps just as well since the 315 reverted to mechanical brakes, the 303's hydraulics never having earned the confidence of customers, who remained suspicious of fragile connections, perishing rubber hoses and corrosive fluid. They happily put up instead with the stretchy cables, clumsy rods and heavy pedal pressures of mechanical systems.

The basis of the BMW range still consisted of conservatively shaped saloons and coupés; it was still too early for rivalry with the great sporting marques such as Vittorio Jano's fine overhead camshaft Alfa Romeos or the handsome Type 57, straight-eight, 95mph Bugattis. BMWs were more properly matched against contemporary saloon Lancias, Citroëns, Opels or Peugeots. Although they were not yet in the sporting league, when they did join it, they came in with a flourish.

Simplicity and reliability distinguished the little Dixi, and the tough little A-frame chassis supported a number of different body styles. Vans await delivery to the German post office, with spare tyres and roofrack to give more room for payload.

It was not the German *autobahn*, but the Italian *autostrada* that pointed the way towards faster inter-city travel. The preliminary stretches had been authorized as far back as 1925, to link Milan and Cremona, and Brescia and Verona. Later plans embraced all the major centres of Italy, and, by 1932, 387 miles (623km) were open. The longest continuous stretch connected Turin with Milan and Brescia, 136 miles (219km) of unbroken motor road, not by any means all dual carriageway, but mostly lit at night and, by Mussolini's time, self-financing through tolls.

The *routes nationales* of France remained much as Napoleon had left them. There were long straight roads in America, but the Pennsylvania Turnpike would not open until 1940. In Britain, motorways would remain a dream for another twenty years. But in Germany things were changing; not all, as it turned out, for the better, but there were the beginnings of a road network that would be an example to the rest of the world.

By the time Germany opened the first inter-city *autobahn* in 1932, from Bonn to Cologne, Italy had traffic running on 330 miles (531km) of *autostrada*, and designers found themselves faced with a new challenge. They had now to build cars capable of cruising at, or close to, top speed in reasonable comfort, in safety, and without coming to pieces or wearing themselves out in the process.

A premium would henceforward be put on speed, together with aspects of roadworthiness that had hitherto been regarded as exclusive to sports or racing cars. Passenger cars would now need to sustain a mile a minute (100kph) for hours on end. They would

# THE
## CLASSIC
## YEARS

1936 – 39

BMW 335. The largest pre-war BMW, only 410 were made up to 1941, when materials shortages forced them to be delivered without tyres, – customers had to find their own.

*Grosser England-Sieg der BMW*

BAYERISCHE MOTOREN WERKE A.G. MÜNCHEN 13

Closely following Henne's triumph at Nürburgring, three BMW 328s were entered in the 1936 Tourist Trophy race by AFN Ltd, painted green for the occasion, driven by 'B Bira', AFP Fane, and HJ Aldington. Fane finished third overall, the cars dominated the 2 litre class, and won the team prize in drenching rain.

need better braking and steering. New qualities would have to be discovered with which only the most inventive engineers would be familiar, and which could best be tested in the heat of motoring competition.

Germany in the 1930s witnessed some of the most progressive automobile engineering in the world, and while Mercedes-Benz and Auto Union were overwhelming the opposition in Grand Prix racing, each tier of motor sport underneath was ready to follow suit.

The rakish appearance of the Sport-Cabriolet 315 had already established the pattern of sports BMWs to come. A two-seater cabriolet version had been made, in small numbers, with wind-up windows and the spare tyre concealed under a neat door in the sweeping tail.

BMW's first proper sports car, however, was the 315/1 Sport, made between 1934 and 1936, with a three-carburettor, 6.8:1 compression version of the 1490cc, six-cylinder engine. The company gave an undertaking that the model would do 120kph (75mph), and some were tuned, enabling them to go even faster. The Sport featured cutaway doors, and spatted rear wheels. A fixed-head version was designed and a prototype built, but never put into production, much as William (later Sir William) Lyons was then doing with the SS (later SS Jaguar) 100 in Britain.

Among the options offered on the 315/1 Sport was a leather strap on the bonnet, as demanded by the Le Mans sports car regulations, indicating that cosmetic sporting attachments were not new even in 1935.

From the 315/1 Sport, it was but a short

step to the 319/1 Sport, with the same triple solex carburettor set-up in the 1911cc, pushrod overhead-valve engine, giving it a top speed of 80mph (129kph). With long-distance *autobahn* journeys no doubt in mind, BMW increased the fuel tank capacity from forty to fifty litres, and at the Berlin Motor Show of 1935 exhibited the car with elongated headlights of the sort that American designers were making fashionable.

The Sport kept most of the touring and saloon cars' mechanical features, such as the transverse-leaf independent front suspension, which had been developed and refined to a point where it was among the best of its type. The front wheels were well located at the top by the leaf-spring, and at the bottom by a tubular wishbone whose widely spaced pivots made the fitting of a torsion bar (which is only a coil spring straightened out to make it fit the available space) a logical development.

Using a sports car for sport was an engaging activity for Freiherr Alex von Falkenhausen, whose career as a competitor and an engineer was connected with BMW throughout his life. Born in the Schwabing district of Munich in 1907, von Falkenhausen did not follow the military vocation of his Prussian ancestors. Instead, by 1930 he had graduated from Munich's Technische Hochschule with an engineering degree. Like many young men of his era, he became passionately involved with motorcycle racing, first with a DKW 125 in 1924 and later with an Alfa-Villiers 175. However, success did not come until he started riding a British Calthorpe in 1932.

'It was so quick that BMW noticed me and in 1934 offered me a works machine,' he told BMW(GB)'s Chris Willows in one of the last interviews he gave before he died at the age of 82 in 1989. 'It seemed to be a good idea to become an engineer for BMW. It was rather difficult at the time because there was a deep depression – no money. It was very kind of them.'

Falkenhausen became a chassis engineer under Director Schleicher, who designed both the first BMW motorcycle in 1923 and the famous BMW 328. Alongside his engineering work he continued to ride BMWs in long trials, winning gold medals in the International Six Days Trials in 1934, 1935 and 1937.

'At the end of 1934 I bought one of the Alpine Rally works cars – a 315/1.' It was this car that so surprised the Frazer Nash 'chain gang' in the 1934 Alpine Rally, and led the Aldington brothers to sell them in Britain under the title Frazer Nash BMW.

'I was very happy with the car. At the time it was a very modern sports car and I did some races and long-distance driving such as the Alpine Trial. Two years later I bought a 319/1 and, in 1939, a 328. That was the real thing. In relation to other cars of the period it had much better roadholding, it was very light, and had a powerful engine with a great deal of torque.'

Sports BMWs were still produced in relatively small numbers however: 242 of the 315/1, and only 102 of the 319/1, while the 319 saloons and tourers were produced by the thousand – 6,543 of the 319 between 1935 and 1937, and 9,521 of the 315. The volumes

generated useful profits, and BMW was ready to move up-market, making all models more obviously sporting, and at the Berlin Motor Show of February 1936 the company stand showed the first 326.

By the summer it was in production, providing the basis for a series of classic cars which secured BMW's reputation for the 1930s, and gave the marque a status that would see it through the upheaval of war with its name and reputation undimmed.

The new order began, as so often in BMW history, with an interim model using some of the features of the new without relinquishing all of those from the old. This was the 329, which temporarily dispensed with BMW's logical numbering system, because it was not a 2.9 litre 3-Series, but merely a No. 2 version of a 319. It had the same engine and chassis, while the styling, with more rounded wings, and a softer

The first BMW sports car. The BMW works team of new 315/1 two-seaters climbs the Stilfser Joch (2,727m) in the 1934 Alpine Trial. Their performance so impressed the Aldingtons that they immediately wrote to Munich asking to be appointed sales agents in Britain.

curve round the bonnet and grille, predicted the shape of things to come.

The 329 was also provided with a separate luggage boot, just big enough to take full-sized suitcases for those long holiday trips that the *autobahn* would doubtless make possible. Access to it was from inside the car, by folding down the rear seat back – not easy, but less difficult than in some contemporaries which offered little more than a fold-down grid arrangement at the back. The spare wheel was enclosed under a separate cover accessible from the outside.

Less than 1,200 examples of the 329 were built during twelve months in 1936–37, phasing in the introduction of a model that would come to be regarded as a major landmark. By the time the 326 was ready for the market, the body had been in production for a year – the saloons from Ambi-Budd, the cabriolets from Autenrieth – and the engine was a development of the trusty six-cylinder, bored out by 1mm to give a capacity of 1971cc.

The major change was the chassis, which was a boxed ladder-style frame instead of being made from welded tubes. There were hydraulic brakes, and the four-speed Hurth gearbox incorporated a freewheel in first and second gears. This was a useful gadget, which enabled the driver to coast through town traffic with the engine idling and not acting as a brake, and make clutchless gearchanges at slow speeds. The rear axle used torsion bar springs for the first time.

The 326 was not a sports car. It was a fairly large, comfortable touring car that would do 72mph (116kph), taking over

half a minute to reach 60mph (100kph). Twenty seconds was not regarded as specially swift in 1936 (by the 1990s anything over ten seconds would be regarded as rather slow), so the 326's acceleration was leisurely by any standards.

Not so BMW's next, graceful new car. While the 326 was brewing, as it were, BMW engineers were at work following up the success of the 319/1 Sport, and while the 326 was introduced in the ordinary course of events at the Berlin Motor Show in 1936, the 328 would make its debut more spectacularly, on the track.

With nothing like the budget of Daimler-Benz and Auto Union, BMW was to make an entrance into motor racing that was hardly less significant. The 328 turned up at the Nürburgring, Germany's showpiece motor racing circuit in the Eifel Mountains, where the 14.7-mile Nordschleife and the 4.8-mile Sudschleife contained 172 corners of infinite variety, 88 left-handed, 84 right-handed, diving and curving through the wooded, rolling countryside.

The date was 14 June 1936, the event was the annual Eifelrennen, and the driver Ernst Henne. At the wheel of a car that would be on sale within months, Henne was entered in the class for unsupercharged cars up to 2 litres in a race which included 1½ litre *racing* cars. To everyone's astonishment, in his (by comparison) almost silent sports car, he led the race, together with Count Trossi's racing Maserati.

Henne won at an average of 63mph (101kph) over the 70 miles (113km), from an Adler which was nearly 3mph slower. Henne's car was a lightweight

AFP Fane wins the 2 litre class in the 1938 Mille Miglia driving a works 328. An accomplished 328 driver, Fane also won at the Nürburgring, and set a new record for the Grossglockner Hill-Climb.

Opposite and following pages: although BMW made only 462 examples of the 328, it featured heavily in the firm's advertising and promotion. Still a flagship, the BMW Museum cherishes this carefully restored sample.

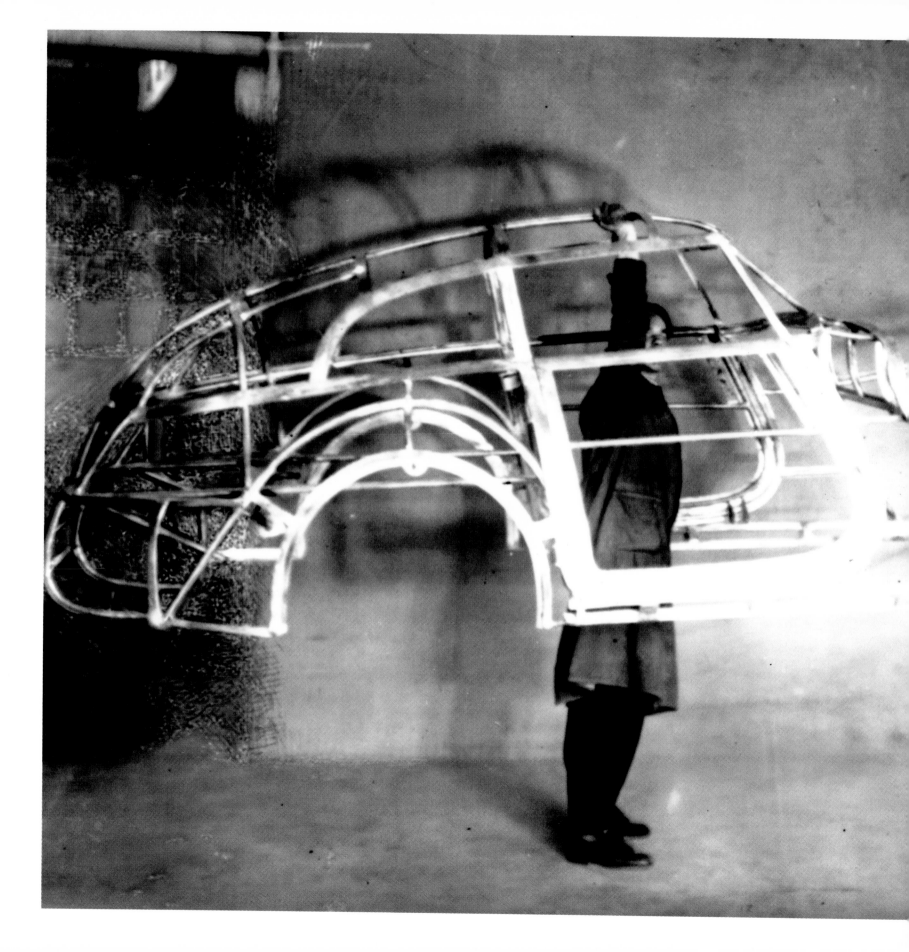

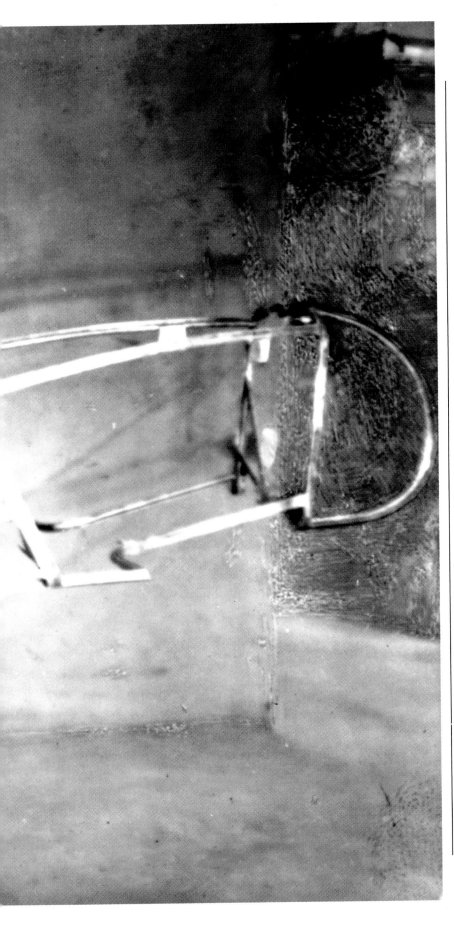

prototype. If the customers had not arrived it could have been quietly withdrawn and the hand-built small-series production stopped.

But the demand was there all right, and sufficient orders came in to allow series-production of properly equipped 328s with real doors and hoods. Jaguar went through the same process of lightweight aluminium-bodied prototypes, to test the market, with the XK120 thirteen years later.

Once again the BMW evolutionary process had achieved an outstanding product. The best ingredients of several models were brought together into one, superb recipe. The nimble, light 319 provided the tubular chassis, the live rear axle, and the transverse-leaf independent front suspension mounted on a welded box structure where the chassis tubes narrowed. BMW was good at welding; it was used instead of bolting the frame together to achieve the stiffness necessary to go with new, supple springing. The cylinder block and the hydraulic brakes came from the new 326. The body was based on the 319/1 but rounded off like the 329, with the distinctive kidney-form grille, and the headlamps sunk into the cowling.

The 328 had knock-off hubs, but the wheels were not the traditional wire-spoked wheels, they were discs, the windscreen was split in the middle, and either side could be folded flat. The car's most distinctive features were the very antithesis of sports cars of the day, which were cramped, uncomfortable and draughty, with a chassis which flexed and a scuttle which shook.

That, said the zealots, was how sports

The lightweight bodies of the 1940 Mille Miglia cars were built from a spidery frame of small tubes with a Duralumin skin. None weighed more than 650 kilograms.

47

cars were supposed to be. The fact of the matter was that light weight and a stiff chassis were still barely compatible. Engineers could still only design strength by having a chassis with beam sections more appropriate to bridge structures than cars. Fast cars had to have large, powerful engines to draw the weight; large engines needed large cars, and large cars were heavy.

Design was a guessing game in which strength was sacrificed for lightness. Good roadholding and handling were achieved principally by bolting the springs up tight, which, with chassis frames weakened in the search for light weight, caused the frames to twist and bend. Consequently, lightweight bodies buckled and came apart at the seams, aluminium cracked and chafed, doors fitted badly, and sports cars rattled.

Turning the equation on its head, and designing a sports car with a stiff chassis and flexible springs instead of the other way round was almost inconceivable, yet that was how the BMW 328 was. The traditional riveted or bolted structures were abandoned, and the chassis was made of tubes fabricated from sheet steel, welded and properly braced, the section varying according to the degree of local stress.

No detail was overlooked. The leather bonnet strap was equipped with special 'over-centre' clips, instead of big belt buckles that would have been slow to undo at a pit stop. Every 328 driver was made to feel that he just might make it to Le Mans and that, when he did, his pit crew would have the best equipment for the job.

The supple suspension not only made

the car ride more smoothly than any sports car of the day, it improved road grip as well, by keeping the tyres constantly in touch with the surface. Instead of bouncing over bumps or leaning on corners, with the tyre contact patch constantly squirming and changing shape, and thus grip, the tyres did their job constantly and consistently.

The 328's steering, a precise rack and pinion arrangement, was light and precise; you did not need to heave a 328's steering, except perhaps at parking speeds. Braking and traction were in a class of their own; the driver had more feel of the road, and on 1936 roads, less smooth than they came to be, he was not so continuously jolted in his seat that he had to steady himself by gripping the steering-wheel. The 328 had the quietness and refinement of a touring car.

Sports car enthusiasts were suspicious, but the evidence of its performance in racing could not be ignored. The 328 was no effete tourer, but a high-performance sports car capable of well over 90mph (150kph), with lively acceleration and, as a result of its light weight and well-shaped body, commendable economy. The large, blunt, ponderous sports cars now consigned to a past era had been heavy to drive and heavy on fuel.

Yet the 328 was more than simply an outstanding chassis and a pretty body. At its heart lay a brilliant engine which had not been designed from the ground up but, in the now customary BMW style, evolved from previous models. The basis was the bottom half of the old six-cylinder 1971cc unit, whose ancestry went back to the 1.2

litre 303, itself based on the old four-cylinder AM4, which was in turn an overhead-valve conversion on the side-valve Austin Seven.

Since the time of Ernest Henry's 1912 Peugeot Grand Prix engine, itself a pirated Hispano-Suiza, engineers have agreed that the most satisfactory shape for a combustion chamber is hemispherical, with the valves splayed at a wide angle, on opposite sides. The best way to achieve this, as Henry and many designers discovered, was to drive the valves by means of two camshafts right at the top of the engine, where they needed to be driven by chains or gears or, more recently, by toothed belt.

In the 1930s, these overhead drives were expensive and invariably noisy, with the wide clearances and loose fit imposed by the machining techniques of the time. Whirring chains and thrashing gears, the problem of getting enough oil to the upper part of the engine, and the complication and power losses of driving two camshafts instead of one, defeated many engineers.

Rudolf Schleicher worked on the original 303 six-cylinder engine under the direction of the Chief Designer, Fritz Fiedler, who took over responsibility for the 326 at Eisenach following its uncertain results with the earlier cars. Schleicher remained in Munich, working principally on engines, and when it came to developing the 2 litre six for a high-performance car, he conceived a novel arrangement to give it inclined overhead valves without the complication of an extra camshaft.

Schleicher took the existing cylinder

block, used the camshaft on the left side to operate the six inlet valves by pushrods as before, then through small rockers running on a shaft in the aluminium cylinder head and a series of short transverse pushrods, worked the exhaust valves. For sheer economy of method it was brilliant. The valves were at an included angle of ninety degrees and the combustion chamber was a classical hemisphere.

There were snags. The spark plugs were located centrally, and buried among the inlet passages, so access was not easy. Getting at them required a special jointed tool and, on a hot engine, plug changes were a slow and bruising business. It was also a tall engine, because the downdraught carburettors had to be mounted above the inlet tracts, leading vertically downwards.

The result was an exemplary, 80 horsepower sports car engine, which would rev freely to 4,500rpm (4,750, it was recommended, should be used for short periods only), with a compression ratio of 7.5:1. It could be made even higher with special pistons which enabled racing engines to run on the 80-octane fuel then becoming available. It was a far cry from the 319's 45 horsepower at 3,750rpm, or even the 319/1's 55 horsepower at 4,000rpm.

The 328 abounded in novel features, some of which only became regular equipment on sports cars many years later, such as the effective hood and sidescreens, whose security was helped by the stiff chassis body structure. Other items, such as the fully-fitted undertray to improve the aerodynamics of a notoriously disorderly region of a car,

Rudolph Schleicher. Together with Fritz Fiedler, Schleicher was responsible for the ingenious valvegear which transformed the six cylinder, 2 litre BMW into the power unit for the remarkable 328.

remained unusual on anything but out-and-out racers.

Two prototype 328s were built in 1936, with lightweight aluminium bodies and no doors. The first batch were also lightweight racers, intended to create the reputation necessary to establish BMW as manufacturers of notable, high-performance cars. The production cars, complete with doors, hood, and an extremely high level of comfort and equipment, were available by the end of the summer of 1936.

It was a model whose reputation would not be dimmed by the passing of time. The 328 remained a competitive 2 litre car for years after the war. In the late 1940s it gave some famous drivers, including Stirling Moss, their first taste of motor racing, while the achievements of the engine became the stuff of motor racing legend.

The 328 was also a car whose distinguished reputation was out of proportion to its numbers. It was soon acknowledged as one of the definitive sports cars of the first half of the century, but of the 462 328s made between 1936 and 1940, fewer than two hundred survived into the second half.

Meanwhile, the commercial business of making cars went on, with the rather plain 320, which was a shortened 326 – something of a bargain at 4,500 Reichsmarks, compared with RM7,400 for a 328, but not if you happened to be in a hurry, since it could only manage 68mph (110kph). More fashionable was the 327, a sporty 2 + 2 326, which was a handsome car on the short wheelbase of the 320, but with a little more power – not much more, for

The sloping tail of the 315 concealed the spare wheel under a hinged cover, and the hood, neatly folded beneath a tonneau cover.

78mph (125kph) was thought of as a useful turn of speed in 1937–38 – and with lines that were regarded as very dashing.

By the time Germany annexed the Sudetenland, Europe was left in little doubt that war was inevitable. The lengthy prelude was brought to an end after Hitler's invasion of Poland in September 1939, and the old order in Europe was changed for ever.

However undesirable war was, it promised swift growth for an industrial enterprise like BMW. By virtue of making aero engines, the company was an arms manufacturer and a fellow-traveller on the Reich's path rather than the navigator of its own fortune. There seemed no reason to doubt the Führer's belief that the conflict would be short-lived, and commercial life, therefore, might expect to continue with little change.

Soon after war was declared, the sale of cars was forbidden, but BMW carried on production at Eisenach in the hope that things would change. At first, deliveries had to be approved by the military authorities, then free sales were once again permitted on all but four-seat cabriolet models ordered by the *Wehrmacht*. The result was that 7,610 cars were made in 1939, very little fewer than the record year of 1936, when 8,847 BMWs emerged from Eisenach. By 1940 production had been reduced to 1,500, and the last 253 BMW cars for more than a decade left the factory in 1941. By the time it was apparent that the war would last longer than the Reich's theoreticians had fore-cast, shortages of metals, fuel and tyres determined the fate of the private car.

Baron Huschke von Hanstein and Walter Baümer, winners of the 1940 Mille Miglia with the architect of their victory, BMW Technical Director, Fritz Fiedler.

Before production stopped, however, motor sport still lay within the remit of German car-makers. During the late 1930s, the Nationalsozialistisches Kraftfahr Korps (NSKK), the Nazi sporting propaganda movement, encouraged BMW to contest international sports car events in the hope of matching the Mercedes-Benz and Auto Union control of Grand Prix racing. The 328 responded with an impressive number of victories, including class wins at Le Mans, the Mille Miglia, and Britain's Tourist Trophy. The Reich's reputation for technical feats was a valuable part of the propaganda offensive that was an essential element in the march to war.

Recalling the increased presence of the Nazi propagandists at races, Freiherr Alex von Falkenhausen remembers the 1940 Mille Miglia victory by the special BMW 328. 'This car was not liked much by the factory. Racing was a separate department under Ernst Loof, who used his experience to race the BMW-based Veritas cars after the war, and the cars were made to the order of the NSKK. They wanted to have a competitive sports car from BMW. It was a national thing – it was not about sport at all.'

The 2 litre class of the 1938 Mille Miglia was won by a more or less production 328, and, as a portent of things to come in the years after the war, it also won its class in the 24 Hours race at Spa-Francorchamps. But Le Mans was already the world's greatest sports car race, and in 1939 the NSKK entered three 328s, one with a lightweight frame and a sleek, aerodynamic coupé body styled and built by Superleggera Touring of Milan. It was a masterpiece of clean aerodynamic design. Modern research has shown it to have a drag coefficient of only 0·30 – the figure modern aerodynamicists regard as close to the practical minimum for a road-going saloon.

The coupé and two open cars were opposed in the 2 litre class by a solitary Aston Martin, so an award of some sort was at least on the cards.

The Aston struggled towards the finish on three cylinders, but the BMWs ran strongly, and not only won the class, but the 2 litre Schaumberg-Lippe-Wenscher coupé finished fifth, only 103 miles behind the winning 3.3 litre Bugatti. The Roese-Heinemann BMW was seventh, and the Brien-Scholz car ninth. All the cars ahead of them were of much larger capacity: a 3 litre Delage, two 4½ litre Lagondas, and two 3½ litre Delahayes.

The Lippe-Wenscher car came second in the Index of Performance to – not very surprisingly since the French invariably managed to contrive a home win in this curious category – a 1.1 litre Simca. More significantly, however, the fifth-placed and class-winning car also managed a big improvement on the previous year's record for the 2 litre class, raising the average speed from 120.7kph (74.8mph) to 132.8kph (82.3mph).

Italy was another target for the propaganda campaign. Still neutral, or 'non-belligerent' in Mussolini's phrase, during the early part of the war, it planned a 1940 edition of the Mille Miglia. Recalling, perhaps a little wistfully, the Tripoli Grand Prix of 1939, for which the Italians had changed the rules in the hope of an easy victory in their new North African Empire, the NSKK was looking for another opportunity to humiliate *Il Duce*.

The Italians ran the Tripoli race for 1½ litre cars instead of the usual 3 litres, to enable their 158 Alfa Romeos to win. Their hopes were dashed when Mercedes-Benz rushed through a new 1½ litre V8, the W 165, which crushed the Alfa Romeos and Maseratis, finishing first and second. Something similar was expected in the Mille Miglia, for which BMW developed new cars to compete not just for a class win, but for outright victory.

The Mille Miglia, literally the 1,000 Mile race, had been a classic in the sporting calendar ever since its inception in 1927. Normally it was run from Brescia down the western side of Italy to Rome, then across the Appennines and back north up the Adriatic coast, through Pesaro and Rimini to Bologna and Brescia. It had always been a challenging route, but in 1938 there was a bad accident in which ten spectators died.

Accordingly it was cancelled in 1939, and in April 1940, titled the Gran Premio di Brescia della Mille Miglia, it was run on a shorter course. The traditional Brescia start remained, but it ran to Cremona, and Mantua, and back to Brescia on a 104-mile triangular circuit. Going round it nine times ensured that it lived up to the name and reputation of the Mille Miglia.

Sports car racing had been the preserve of French and Italian cars through much of the previous decade, so it was specially important for Germany to demonstrate to its partner in the Pact of Steel that its cars and drivers could dominate in any class it chose, even more than seven months into the war.

Le Mans, 1939. The two open BMW 328s driven by Roese and Heinemann, and Brien and Scholz finished 7th and 9th behind the coupé of Prince Schaumburg-Lippe and Wenscher in 5th place.

The stylish open two seater BMW of Wencher and Scholtz passes the grandstand and race control tower at Brescia, on the Mille Miglia. It finished in 6th place.

Using Schleicher's brilliant 328 as a base, BMW prepared, at the NSKK's behest, a three-pronged attack run by team manager Ernst Loof. Fine tuning the engine produced a reliable 120 bhp on alcohol fuel, 50 per cent more than the standard production engine, but the real difference lay in the bodywork.

In the circumstances, it was hardly fitting for BMW to use an Italian body, but for Le Mans, with so little time in which to develop one, it had proved expedient. For the Mille Miglia, BMW developed its own coupé which, while sharing the lightweight frame construction of the Superleggera Touring Le Mans car, looked quite different.

Inspired by the German school of aerodynamic theory led by Dr Wunibald Kamm, the high-tailed, bulbous machine lacked the elegance of the Italian design, yet it belied its looks, and proved the quickest of the five BMWs entered, reaching 135mph on the straight. Unfortunately, the engine did not work very well, and it

became the only one of the team to retire.

The Touring Coupé driven by Huschke von Hanstein and Walter Baumer won the race at an average speed of 104mph (166.2kph). The favourites, Alfa Romeo, were beaten both for outright pace and consistency, and Farina finished fully fifteen minutes behind the BMW. The less aerodynamic but lighter BMW open cars were also quicker than the Alfas which, with 2.4 litres and overhead camshaft engines, had been expected to be much faster.

Curiously, the sports BMWs which finished third, fifth and sixth are the cars with which the names Mille Miglia and BMW have become emotionally linked. They were outstandingly pretty and made everything else look hopelessly dated. Their flowing wings blended with the bonnet and boot line, anticipating the appearance of the post-war sports car ten years later. Sir William Lyons certainly took a long, hard look at the Mille Miglia BMW before designing the classic 1948 Jaguar XK120.

All three roadsters survived, one in BMW's own museum, one in the United States, and one in Riga. In 1945 H. J. Aldington of AFN, the British importers before the war, rescued one. He returned to Germany ostensibly to reclaim his own 328, which had been left in Munich since before the war, but returned instead with one of the open Mille Miglia cars which was handed over as much to protect it from the depredations of the occupying forces as anything else.

It was later equipped with a Frazer Nash radiator and displayed to an unquestioning press as a prototype of a new model. Later still, it was raced in Britain by Gilbert Tyrer, then acquired by Michael Bowler, before being restored and returned to Germany.

The winning coupé of Huschke von Hanstein and Walter Baumer also survived and went to the United States. Of the other cars, only the squared-off coupé has been lost to history.

The 328 Mille Miglia cars and their classic engine may have had their own profound effect upon post-war car development, but it was BMW's last public triumph for many years. Its importance was the niche it carved in the annals of motor racing, and the respect it created in the hearts and minds of enthusiasts. It was certainly a milestone in the development of BMW.

The development of racing and sports cars continued behind closed doors during 1940. Touring Superleggera produced an even smoother roadster for the proposed 1941 Mille Miglia, and BMW's development department, under Alex von Falkenhausen, worked on a 2.5 litre, 150bhp twin overhead camshaft engine for it. Unfortunately it never reached production, although one was brought back to England by Aldington when the design of the new Bristol was under consideration.

The next generation of BMWs was also under development as war broke out. The 332 model was a 2 litre version of the 335 with more attractive, and therefore more saleable, Kamm-inspired body styling. It had clean lines, integrated headlights and half-enclosed rear wheels, and it is not hard to imagine it developing during the 1940s along the lines of the BMWs of the Fifties. As it turned out, the 332's

only real claim to fame is that one prototype carried General de Gaulle to Strasbourg after the city fell to France in 1945.

Both the build-up for war and the conflict itself brought huge demands for military vehicles. Even before the military expansion which began in 1935, all manner of light cars and vans were pressed into army service. BMW supplied an estimated two thousand car chassis for communications and staff car duties up to 1937, including several hundred Dixi and 3/15 models. They were never designed for rigorous army use, however, and the *Wehrmacht* specified a new type of *kübelwagen* (literally 'bucket-car') for more serious off-road employment.

BMW became one of three producers to meet the authorities' specification (Stoewer and Hanomag were the others), and this model, known as the 325, would sit happily in a modern car dealer's showroom. Powered by a 50bhp, 1971cc six-cylinder engine, the 325 had four-wheel drive, each axle having a locking differential; there was four-wheel steering, a five-speed gearbox and twin coil springs for each wheel. Between 1937 and 1940 BMW produced 3,225 examples of this specialized vehicle, but not one bore the blue and white badge, which was held in readiness for the return to a troubled peace.

When Gustav Otto set up business in Munich in 1911, the engineering philosophy of aero engines was well ahead of the airframes in which they flew. Engines were already years in advance of the Wright Brothers' frail wings of 1903, and developed fast. Blériot's flimsy cross-Channel monoplane of 1909 only had a 25 horsepower Anzani, which needed a shower of rain to keep it cool, but by the time of the First World War, the redoubtable Dr.-Ing. Ferdinand Porsche had 120 horsepower and six cylinders ready for the Central Powers to use in their fighting aircraft.

Porsche was Technical Director of Austro-Daimler, and it was another of his designs, a V12 with welded steel water jackets, seven main bearings, and inclined pushrod overhead valves, that Castiglioni had negotiated away to Otto and Rapp's Bayerische Flugzeugwerke.

When Friz's BMW III went into production in February 1917, it used welded, not cast, water jackets too, in his quest for lightness and reliability, and had a capacity of 19.08 litres. And to take advantage of the benzole-blended fuel that the hard-pressed Flying Corps was now able to get, it had 6.4:1 compression cylinder heads, to provide extra power for the dog-fights the pilots would soon have to face.

The aviators were advised not to use full throttle until they were well airborne. At low altitudes, the weak mixture in the high-compression engines in the dense atmosphere near the ground would have blown them to pieces. Full power could only be used when the aircraft was flying in thinner air above 2,000

# FLIGHT

AIRCRAFT &

ENGINES

Fernlicht. The inspiration for the later Bristol, the 327/28 BMW had an arc-type speedometer reading up to 160kph (100mph).

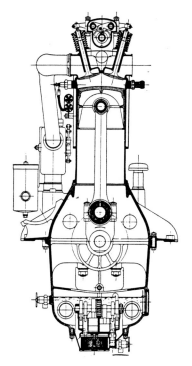

Classic of the skies. The BMW IIIa aero engine with a single gear-driven overhead camshaft operating inclined valves.

metres (6,560 feet), when the extra carburettor throat balanced it out nicely. For take-off, the III gave 185 horse-power, with specially strengthened versions giving 220, at 1,400rpm.

Friz's revised engine, the IIIa, ran in November 1917, but test-pilots were wary of new designs. The only way the young engineer could find anyone willing to fly it, was to show his confidence in it by offering himself up as a passenger. In the event, the IIIa performed convincingly, and the first batch was delivered to von Richthofen's famous Flying Circus. One of its pilots, Ernst Udet, later General-Luftzeugmeister of the *Luftwaffe*, was warm in his praise for an engine that came too late to alter the course of the war, but would make BMW's fortune in times of peace.

It could still produce 120 horsepower at 6,000 metres (nearly 20,000 feet), and

Friz improved even the unpromising Austro-Daimler V12 to make it give 370 horsepower at 5,000 metres (16,400 feet). By the end of the war, BMW was making 150 engines a month.

The Air Clauses of the Treaty of Versailles demanded that nearly all the 20,000 aircraft of the German Flying Corps be dismantled. Some 15,000 planes and 27,000 engines, many of them BMW IIIas in aircraft such as the nimble Fokker DVII of the Jagdgeschwader Richthofen, were surrendered, and the Allies ordered that aero-engine plants should also be made inoperable. One of the conditions imposed by the Treaty, which would become such a contentious issue in Germany in years to come, was that the machinery on which the engines had been made should also be broken up.

A large number of connecting-rods was

No. 4 Wing of Baron von Richthofen's pursuit squadron Jagdgeschwader 1, awaits to get airborne. On the right, without cap is Ernst Udet, Flight Lieutenant and accomplished pilot.

included in the demolition order, but BMW had other plans for them. The Allied Technical Commission had demanded they be destroyed by crushing. Accordingly BMW technicians carefully made up pressure dies to exactly the right dimensions, and the rods were solemnly placed in the press tools – and removed undamaged.

A new engine was illicitly constructed, with the double-pressed con-rods, fitted in a DFW C IV biplane, and on 9 May 1919 Lieutenant Zeno Diemer reached an altitude of 9,700 metres (31,826 feet). On 17 June he went even higher, to 9,760 metres (32,023 feet) inside 87 minutes' flying time, but the new record was never officially ratified, because Germany's membership of the Fédération Aéronautique Internationale (FAI) had lapsed following the war. Only the absence of an oxygen system prevented the gallant Diemer from reaching 10,000 metres (32,810 feet),

and within a year, on 20 February 1920, Major R. W. Schroeder had set the official ceiling at 33,113 feet (10,518 metres) in a Lapere at Dayton, Ohio.

In the confusion and political void of Germany at the dawn of the 1920s, BMW had to fight hard in order to survive. The altitude record was an act of defiance at a time when German industry was being dismembered. The technical drawings, plans and prototypes of the BMW IV had to be given up to the Allied Technical Commissioners, and BMW had to make something – anything – to keep going.

Yet the Allies largely overlooked the role that air power would play in the years to come. By 1922 civil aircraft production was sanctioned again, and the Paris Air Agreement of 1926 effectively opened the way for Germany to become the most air-minded nation in Europe. Commercial aviation expanded, flying clubs were formed, and as early as 1920 a far-sighted General Hans von Seeckt laid the foundations of a new Air Force. He filled the ranks of his Ministry of Defence with aviation experts who could plot the establishment of a new aircraft industry.

Within a few years Junkers had set up business in Dessau, Heinkel at Warnemünde on the Baltic, and Dornier in the old Zeppelin sheds at Friedrichshafen. Heinrich Focke and Georg Wulf went into partnership as the Focke-Wulf Flugzeugbau in a Bremen cellar, and from the ruins of the Udet-Flugzeugbau at Augsburg came another Bayerische Flugzeugwerke (a different one from the company of the same name – one of BMW's parents) which became Messerschmitt AG.

All would become customers of BMW, for new engines coming from the works at Moosacher Strasse, looking pretty much like the old ones that had only just been handed over to the Allied Control Commission. They were still the water-cooled, six-cylinder III, and the first aircraft they flew in were based on the fighters that the Allies had only recently confiscated – except that they were rather better. A new aviation age was dawning for the new, air-minded generation.

But there was also to be a new series of water-cooled engines, all based on the same six-cylinder that had shown itself so reliable and strong. Helmut Sachse led the team responsible for them, starting with the BMW IV, another straight six-cylinder, and the V of 1926, a V12, which was effectively two IIIa units mounted on a common

crankcase, giving between 360 and 420 horsepower. The BMW VI was much the same, two doubled-up IVs, with the connecting-rods of each opposing cylinder running on the same crankpins of the roller-bearing crankshaft, to keep the length of the engine much the same as that of the six-cylinder. Giving between 500 and 750 horsepower, the VI became one of the most significant engines of the inter-war years.

The VI was nearly 47 litres in capacity, with large cylinders developing up to 440 horsepower, and over 9,000 were built up to 1938. It powered Germany's growing civil aviation industry, and was also used for the first aircraft under development for the new *Luftwaffe*. The BMW IV was licensed for production abroad, and was made in substantial numbers as the M-17 in the Soviet Union, succeeding the venerable M-5 Liberty as the standard V12 of the Soviet air force.

The BMW VI was built in large numbers for the new German civil aircraft, and among the Russian transports that used the M-17 was a 1932 version of the ANT-9 from the Tupolev Design Office. Designed with three engines, it turned out to be faster with two BMWs. The total of M–17s and the later AM-30s made in the Soviet Union may never be known, but the VI was used in a wide variety of aircraft, made in substantial numbers.

Under the Treaty of Rapallo, the fledgeling *Luftwaffe* trained illicitly in the Soviet Union at Lipetsk, well away from the surveillance of the Versailles powers. It flew Junkers F13s, with BMW IV engines, which also formed the basis

Max Friz, second from right with test pilot Zeno Diemer after his record-breaking flight.

BMW compares Diemer's new altitude record of 11 May 1919 with the Zugspitse, Mont Blanc, and Everest.

of Dobroljot, the Soviet airline which became Aeroflot.

The F13, of 1919, was an advanced all-metal cantilever-wing monoplane at a time when most of its contemporaries were fabric-covered biplanes in which the wind whistled through the bracing wires and pilots froze in open cockpits. Junkers F13 pilots flew in an enclosed cabin, and the fuselage was covered in the distinctive tough, ribbed duralumin, extremely suitable for all-weather aircraft, that was to be a characteristic of the later, exemplary Junkers 52.

The F13 remained in production until 1932, and most of the 350 built had BMW IIIa and IV engines. Together, they opened up air routes all over the world, and led to the family of Junkers aircraft such as the W34, which flew in 1926, initially with a Gnome-Rhône radial, and later a BMW 132A nine-cylinder licence-built Hornet. The W34 not only pioneered airline operations for Lufthansa, but over 900 of them flew with the *Luftwaffe* in the Second World War, the last one still flying in 1962.

Another early client for the IIIa was the 1921 Dornier Komet, which contravened the Versailles Treaty, because its 185 horsepower BMW enabled it to fly higher and faster than the Treaty's Air Clauses allowed. With seats for four passengers, the Komet launched Deutsche Luft-Reederei and Deutscher Aero Lloyd, which became Luft Hansa in 1926.

By 1925, as the Treaty relaxed its grip, the Komet's successor, the Merkur, could fly as high and as far as it liked. With a 600 horsepower BMW VI it carried six passengers at 180kph (112mph), and Deutsche Lufthansa put

BMW revived the Wartburg title for a sporting version of the Dixi, with 18 horsepower against the standard car's 15. The DA3 or Wartburg Sport was made in 1930–31.

Pioneering flights to far-flung corners of the world included those of BMW-powered Dornier Merkur floatplanes across Africa in 1926. This stop was by Lake Tanganyika.

36 into service on long international routes, such as the one between Berlin and Moscow. Its most notable exploit took place between 7 December 1926 and 21 February 1927, when Walter Mittelholzer of the Swiss army flew one from Zürich to Capetown.

In a newly-built Merkur, Mittelholzer flew the 20,000km (12,400 miles) in 97½ hours with a mechanic, two scientists, cameras and darkroom equipment, the crew's tents and other supplies for overnight stops, and '. . . weapons in case of possible accidents' on board. He arrived at Capetown at 05.00, after an exhausting trip, and wasted no time in dispatching, at 08.20, a telegram in English to Bayern motor München: 'Congratulate your engines wonderful all through. Mittelholzer.'

He must have been a determined pilot. In 1924 he flew a Junkers Ju20 with a BMW IV engine from Zürich to Teheran in 41 hours, carrying a 1,600lb (735kg) cargo, reaching an altitude of 6,000 metres (19,700 feet).

Another aircraft technically in breach of the Versailles Treaty was the Dornier Wal, a seaplane which first flew in 1922. It was powered by two V12 BMW VI engines of 600 horsepower mounted in a central nacelle above the wing. Dornier neatly circumvented the terms of the Treaty by building the aircraft in Italy, at a subsidiary company, Costruzioni Meccaniche Aeronautiche SA, which made 150 of them.

A total of 300 Wals were built, of which some had Fiat, Napier Lion, or six-cylinder BMW III engines, with which the aircraft had a distinguished record of long-distance flights including an Atlantic crossing in 1930, and exploring the Arctic with the Norwegian, Roald Amundsen. The thousandth BMW VI was produced by 1930, and in 1932 a modified VI was fitted to the Wal in which Wolfgang von Gronau flew 44,800km (27,776 miles) round the world.

Kurt Tank, an engineer with the Rohrbach Metallflugzeugbau, also hit on construction abroad as a means of outflanking the Treaty. His company made aircraft in smoothly finished metal (unlike the corrugated Junkers), and he designed a new flying-boat which would be built in Copenhagen.

The Rohrbach Roma flew in 1929 with three 750 horsepower BMW VI water-cooled V12s on pylons above the wing, not unlike the Wal, with pusher propellors. It was designed to cross the Atlantic with twenty passengers, but in the event proved unsuitable, and went into service on the Baltic instead. Only three aircraft were built, yet the Romar's construction, which came to be a prototype for many all-metal aircraft, and the appointment of its designer to a

The shapely Heinkel He70 Lightning with elliptical wings not unlike the later Spitfire, and a BMW VI engine was Europe's fastest passenger aircraft in 1933.

senior position at Focke-Wulf, secured its place in the long history of aviation.

Another trend-setting record-breaker was the pretty Heinkel He70 of 1932, with its elliptical wooden wings, not unlike a Spitfire's, and streamlined metal fuselage with flush rivetting to make it as slippery as possible. The prototype reached 377kph (234mph) with its BMW VI V12 engine using glycol cooling, to become Europe's fastest aircraft for carrying passengers, even though it could only manage four of them at a time.

The 1930s was the heyday of airliner record-breaking. The new aviation industry was anxious to prove that air travel was not only practical and safe, but would in time become cheap. In 1937 it was Germany's turn with one of the new Junkers Ju90. Alas, the first prototype, *Der Grosse Dessauer*, broke up in flight, but a second, *Bayern*, with four BMW 132 nine-cylinder radials ran on Lufthansa's Berlin to Vienna service in 1938.

The Focke-Wulf Fw 200 Condor was a slim, elegant aircraft, also with four BMW 132 engines, and on 27 June 1938 the prototype, with its designer Kurt Tank and Focke-Wulf's chief test-pilot Hans Sander, flew from Berlin to Cairo via Salonika in record time. On 10 August, Luftansa pilot Alfred Henke flew *Brandenburg*, the first Condor, now redesignated Fw200S-1 and registered D-ACON, non-stop from Berlin to New York in 24 hours 56 minutes and 12 seconds. It returned three days later in 19 hours 55 minutes and 1 second – 45 hours there and back.

The same Condor, D-ACON, emulated the feat on 28 November, by flying from

Berlin to Tokyo, via Basra, Karachi and Hanoi, in 46 hours 18 minutes. It was a promising start to the career of a great aircraft, although it was to gain most of its fame later, when Winston Churchill described it as 'the scourge of the Atlantic'. A few Condors were still flying as late as 1947.

Equipped with guns and bombs, the endurance range of the Condor suited it perfectly for *Luftwaffe* operations against shipping. By September 1940, Condors, mostly flying from bases in France, had sunk 90,000 tons of Allied ships, and it was well into the war before countermeasures such as shipborne fighter aircraft proved effective against them. Aeroplane engine development had been accelerating ever since Hitler finally assumed power in 1935. Following the foundations von Seeckt had created for the new *Luftwaffe*, and the pilot training carried out in Russia, a new generation of aircraft and a new generation of engines were needed.

The Reich's plans for rearmament were

Floyd-Bennett Field, New York, NY, with the record-breaking prototype Focke-Wulf Condor. Its temporary Pratt & Whitney engines were replaced by similar, but slightly less powerful BMW 9 cylinder radials for the Berlin to New York flight. Later Condors had three-bladed propellers.

*Left*: Intended for Lufthansa's Transatlantic service, the Romar was demoted to passenger-carrying on the Baltic routes when it failed to meet its design targets.

The BMW Xa, the small 5 cylinder 2.93 litre radial which BMW made in small numbers in 1927. It was rated at only 68 horse power, but led on to BMW building the Pratt & Whitney Hornet under licence.

clear, and after the difficult years of depression this was good news for an aero engine maker. BMW quickly organized itself to meet the demand. Following a short-lived acquisition by BFW (Messerschmitt), when it became BMW Flugmotorenbau GmbH, BMW began the development of air-cooled radial engines, first the BMW X and Xa, a small five-cylinder of only 2.93 litres. By 1929, however, the well-established short-cut was taken of buying in a licence, and manufacturing somebody else's design.

Company statistics show that it was aero engines which generated BMW's swift growth. In 1932 the low-ebb workforce of 2,800 achieved a turnover of only 19 million Marks. By 1935 the company employed 11,100 people, and turnover had risen nearly sevenfold to 128 million Marks. Such growth was certainly not attributable to car and motorcycle sales, nor to the newly created military equipment division of

Eisenach, where until 1941 BMW built infantry and anti-tank guns, a short-lived venture which lay far from its central business.

The company continued to make the 12-cylinder, water-cooled, in-line VI, but was also now committed to an air-cooled radial. After the difficulties of developing the X and Xa, Franz-Josef Popp negotiated a licence in 1929, with Pratt and Whitney of the United States, to build a ready-made design, the successful new Hornet. This was a 525bhp, nine-cylinder radial, which would be produced in huge numbers not only for the US military, but also for nine out of ten US civil airliners such as the Douglas DC-2.

BMW made sixteen versions of the Hornet, known as the BMW 132, those with the suffix A, E or H running on carburettors, while the rest had direct injection systems, mostly by Bosch. After the occupation, French factories

made a number of 132Ts, swelling the total made by 1945 to over 21,000.

Among the famous aircraft to use the BMW-Hornet-132, besides the Focke-Wulf Condor and the Junkers Ju90, was the Junkers Ju52, the three-engined workhorse of the *Luftwaffe*, used for dropping parachute troops and countless transport tasks. There was even a compression-ignition version, the BMW-Lanova 114 four-stroke diesel developed from the Hornet in 1937, a 650 horsepower engine with liquid-cooled cylinders, each with its own radiator.

BMW refined its Hornet, throughout the 1930s, and indeed throughout the war. By the time production ceased in 1945, around 21,000 examples of the sixteen types had been built, and the power had gone up to 970bhp. It remained a notable engine, but by 1938 the projected high-speed fighters Hitler was planning needed more power.

Moreover, fat air-cooled radials were deemed less satisfactory aerodynamically than slim, in-line Vees.

Governments in other countries have been criticized for delaying their rearmament programme in the 1930s, while Germany grew more formidable. They seemed slow in reacting to the international situation, some with vain hopes that the impending conflict would not happen, some simply unprepared through bureaucratic inertia, a condition from which even Germany was not exempt. Despite a firm commitment from the High Command in Berlin, ineptitude hampered German manufacturers as much as any.

The bureaucrats in the Reichsluftfahrtministerium (RLM, the state air ministry) had decided that there was no future for air-cooled engines, and refused to sanction BMW's request to take up a further licence from Pratt and Whitney for a double row radial. By the time the RLM had reconsidered its position, America would no longer approve arms trading with Germany. Bureaucracy had denied the *Luftwaffe* quick access to useful technology just when it was most needed.

The US Navy, on the other hand, thought so highly of the Hornet that it said it would have no need ever again to buy water-cooled engines. The doubled-up radials made by Pratt and Whitney became among the most successful aircraft engines of all time, 19,000 of them equipping B-24 Consolidated Liberators (ironically the Royal Air Force equivalent of the Condor in U-boat hunting), and 10,000 of them C-47s, to name but two.

The RLM then adopted a policy of promoting competition. BMW would be the principal maker of air-cooled engines, while Daimler-Benz got the water-cooled ones. The days of BMW's big V12 were clearly numbered, and although it continued in production until 1939, the company had to start from scratch, and develop its own air-cooled power units.

The RLM then charged both BMW and the Brandenburgische Motoren Werke (Bramo, a subsidiary of Siemens in Berlin) with the task of competing for the *Luftwaffe's* radial engine. BMW's swift but unsatisfactory answer was to place two 132 units back to back on a single crankcase. The resultant 14-cylinder 139 had a total capacity of 55.4 litres, and developed 1,550bhp when it was tested in 1938.

It suffered from two main problems. It proved difficult to get sufficient air through to cool the rear bank of cylinders, and the frontal area was too large. The fundamental difficulty of a radial engine remained that of fitting it into a streamlined aircraft's nose. The Type 139 was tested in prototypes of the Focke-Wulf 190 fighter, its designer Kurt Tank preferring it to the Daimler-Benz 601 or Jumo 211.

The problem of cooling the rearmost cylinders soon became apparent, and despite the ten-bladed fan inside the cowling running at twice propeller speed, extremely high cockpit temperatures were recorded. On 1 June 1939, when Flugkapitän Hans Sander, Focke-Wulf's chief test-pilot, flew it, he said, 'I felt as though I had my feet in the fireplace.'

The 139 was also tried in the Dornier 217, but BMW dropped it, in favour of a more considered and all-new double row radial. This 14-cylinder unit was the BMW 801, and a marked step forward from the 139. Although it was only 41.8 litres, it produced the same power as the 139, but was a much more compact design which would create significantly less drag.

The 801 used the very latest technology, including supercharging and fuel injection, but the most important innovation was the *Kommandogerät*. This was a mechanical control unit of the utmost complexity, operated by a single lever in the cockpit, which automatically adjusted the fuel flow and mixture control, set the propeller pitch, ignition timing, and also cut in the second stage of the supercharger at the appropriate height. It was, in some respects, a mechanical ancestor, with rods and levers and bell-crank mechanisms built

The Albatros-Werke of Johannistal was one of Germany's foremost manufacturers of military aircraft, many of them with BMW engines. They were flown by aces of the Imperial German Air Service (Luftstreitkräfte) including Rittmeister Manfred, Frieherr von Richthofen, and Hauptmann Oswald Boelcke. Its only rival was the BMW IIIa-engined Fokker D DVIII (page 71) which led to the so-called 'Fokker Scourge' of Allied aircraft in 1915–16.

Popp faces his persecutors. Franz-Josef Popp, under pressure to increase war production with Hitler, Generaloberst von Blomberg of the Wehrmacht General Staff, and General der Flieger Milch, of the German Air Ministry, who later dismissed him.

to watch-making standards, of the electronic engine management system BMW was to pioneer in cars in the late 1970s.

The principal and most noteworthy beneficiary of the 801 engine was still the Focke-Wulf 190, although Tank had to redesign the aircraft round it. The 801 was longer and heavier than the 139, and after trying to accommodate it by moving the cockpit aft, and re-structuring the front, Tank was left with a less manoeuvrable aircraft, and it was necessary to start again.

Accordingly, with bigger wings and an altered tailplane, the 190 V5 emerged, only 6mph slower than it had been, but greatly improved in climb, roll and handling. Overheating remained a problem, even after the aircraft's operational trials began in the summer of 1941 from the air base at Le Bourget in northern France. Engines would seize during flight, or on take-off. Some fifty modifications were found necessary, but the important *Kommandogerät* so improved engine efficiency that the service life between overhauls was increased from 20 to two 200 hours' flying.

The Fw 190 was not in service at the time of the Battle of Britain, so its first clashes with the RAF came in 1941, when it proved to have better handling and performance than the contemporary Spitfire and Hurricane. Yet even the *Kommandogerät* had its weaknesses. The RAF opponents soon discovered that just before the second stage of the supercharger cut in at around 18,000 feet (5,500 metres), their Rolls-Royce Merlins had more power than the BMW. Accordingly, they always tried to engage the Fw 190 at

just below 18,000 feet to make the most of their advantage. Although few 190s survived into old age, more than twenty thousand were made, and development continued right up to 1945.

A number of refinements were built into later versions of the BMW 801, including water methanol and nitrous oxide injection, raising power to 2,270bhp on take-off and 1,715bhp at an altitude of seven miles. More than 60,000 were produced during the years of conflict.

BMW expanded substantially during this period, but it is doubtful that it could have handled such rapid growth on its own. In a move inspired by the RLM, acknowledging that economies of scale would be more likely to achieve high output than competition, BMW took over the Brandenburgische Motoren Werke (Bramo) in 1939 and the result was named BMW Flugmotorenbau GmbH. The merger concerned only aero-engine production, not the car and motorcycle divisions.

The 'A' version of the 801 went into production in 1940, giving 1,600 horsepower. The 802, an 18-cylinder variant, with 2,700 horsepower, was planned, but its development was abandoned in 1942. Once again, the speed of design had passed it by, with one of the most powerful piston aero engines ever, the BMW 803.

This was a 28-cylinder, liquid-cooled engine. In principle it was two 14-cylinder radial units, mechanically independent, mounted back to back. The cylinders in each row were directly behind one another, with each pair sharing a cylinder head and camshaft.

The power from the rear 14 cylinders was transmitted forward through five shafts radially arranged in the crankcase to drive one propeller. This in turn lay directly behind another contra-rotating propeller driven by the front 14 cylinders.

Only a few pre-production engines were built to test different valve systems and other novelties. An 83.5 litre leviathan, the 803 nonetheless showed great promise, producing 4,100bhp for take-off, with a continuous rating of 2,880bhp, but it was never developed to an airworthy state. By the latter part of the war, it became apparent that the piston engine, so far as aircraft were concerned, was approaching its limits in power and complexity.

BMW started research on jet propulsion in 1934, when Kurt Loehner began work on turbochargers for piston engines, in an effort to boost their performance at high altitudes. Loehner's work quickly revealed that driving a very high-speed turbine from the rush of hot exhaust gases could compensate for the thinner air at great heights, but that the heat and pressure it created tended to melt the materials then available.

The RLM was anxious to encourage development of gas turbines to drive propellers and also pure jet engines, in which BMW and Bramo both showed interest. BMW already had turbine experience, and when Bramo was under threat of closure, its management decided they had better do as the ministry told them. Privately, Bramo's Engineering Director Bruno Bruckmann and Research Director Hermann Oesterich doubted whether it could be managed, regarding a ducted fan design as more likely to be successful.

By 1938 small prototypes were being flown, but when the principle was scaled up to provide useful power, the results were disappointing. Ducted fans never lived up to their promise until turbine engines could be employed, and by 1939 Bramo went for the out-and-out turbojet instead.

The only way for Bramo to avoid closure in 1938 was to pool its engineering and design resources, and accept a virtual take-over, under which the BMW aero-engine design office at Munich-Allach carried on its work with its axial compressor turbojet known as the 109/003, while the former Bramo team pursued a counter-rotating centrifugal one, the 109/002.

Hans Rosskopf, the Bramo Chief Designer at Spandau, completed the design work for the production 003A in September 1942, and by the following spring most of the worst problems were overcome. The first flight did not take place until October, when one was mounted under the nose of a Junkers 88 A-5. Reliability remained problematical, but by the end of the year 50 hours' flying between overhauls was guaranteed – not enough for a front-line engine but under war conditions, with so much at stake for Germany, the best that could be achieved.

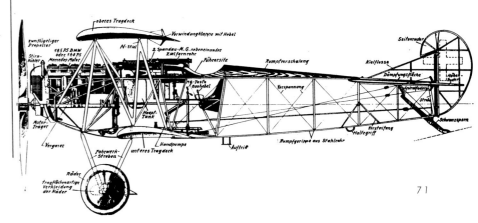

The RLM had sufficient faith in the 003A to back it against the larger Jumo 004B, in the belief that it would eventually be a match for it. Huge resources were put behind it, and by August 1944, a hundred had been delivered. By the end of the war, 1,300 had been made, a quite surprising achievement in view of the shortages of materials, the Allied bombing, and the disastrous course of the war.

Most of the engines were never installed in aircraft, despite plans to produce large numbers of small interceptors, such as the Heinkel He 162, the *Volksjäger*, or Peoples' Fighter, which was rushed from drawing-board to production in a matter of weeks. It was planned to make 4,000 a month, but only a few hundred, hastily assembled, were ready by the time the war ended.

Development of the counter-rotating 002 was abandoned in order to concentrate on the 003, and by mid 1943 the 003A pre-production engine produced a thrust of 1,760lb and was ready for production a year later.

The Jumo 109-004B, a heavier single-shaft axial turbojet, was given the go-ahead to power the Me 262, but the BMW jet was selected for the Arado A234. With four such engines, it was the first jet bomber to see action, and could reach 540mph and fly at 42,000 feet, far above the operational altitudes of its opponents. But it came too late to influence the outcome of the war. The development delays caused by the prevarication of the RLM ensured that the efforts of the engineers to provide a combat jet aircraft amounted to little in the face of the overwhelming force of the Allies.

Large round dials of the 327. Function was more important in 1937 than cosmetic woodwork or contrived trendiness. The long, rather springy gear lever looks un-sporting, yet works crisply enough.

Only two Messerschmitt 262s flew with BMW engines. The first operational jet fighter in history was equipped with Junkers Jumo 004B engines. Yet BMW jets saw service in a variety of Luftwaffe aircraft before the war's end.

Just as there was a bewildering number of piston-engined aircraft projects, so there was a surprising range of jets put in hand. The BMW 003R was a development of the jet engine, with a BMW 718 rocket, burning concentrated nitric acid and self-igniting fuel, to provide 2,700lb of thrust, but it turned out to be dangerously temperamental. In March 1945, a 003R accelerated a Messerschmitt 262 so quickly on take-off, that the pilot thought the flaps and wheels might be torn off before he had time to retract them. It took only 50 seconds to reach 6,000 metres (19,686 feet), and the aircraft carried on to 8,000 metres (26,248 feet) before the rocket fuel was expended.

The 109-028 turboprop and 018 turbojet were planned to give over 7,000lb of thrust, and were almost ready for testing, but never used. More practical were the rocket motors used in air-to-air and ground-to-air missiles, some of which were capable of supersonic flight.

The sheer number of projects in hand at the end of the war proved that an excess of ingenuity is worthless without sufficient resources to execute them. There is no doubt that Germany's engineers had a surfeit of brilliant notions, but they were not well managed by the RLM, and in the end confusion took over, each bright idea in turn imagined as the saviour of the Reich.

Throughout the war, BMW's income rose dramatically. By 1942 the workforce had gone up to 47,300 and turnover was RM560 million, a thirty-fold increase in ten years. Apart from the Munich and Eisenach factories, and the former Bramo plant in Spandau, Berlin, production was carried out in 'shadow factories' outside the main towns. This form of protection, also used in Britain, was to maintain production in the face of the increasing number of bomber attacks. Munich had a shadow facility at Allach, Eisenach had Durrehof, and Spandau had Zuhlsdorf, much of which was underground.

The once small producer of cars and motorcycles was now one of Germany's leading industrial combines, although sadly the architect of its past, and founding father, Franz-Josef Popp, was no longer there to see it. From the mid 1930s, Popp had felt that companies should not grow beyond a size that could be maintained in peacetime. His friendships with Americans, that had led to the Pratt and Whitney deal, and his daughter's marriage to the English racing driver Dick Seaman (who drove and died in a German racing car), did not endear him to the Nazis, and in particular General Milch, head of the RLM.

Delays on engine development angered Milch still further, and when Popp refused to agree production quotas for 1942, despite the company's endeavours, Milch declared him to be a saboteur. Although Popp was threatened with internment at Tilsit concentration camp, or worse, eventually his dismissal sufficed. He returned to his home south of Stuttgart and died in 1954.

Popp's successor was Fritz Hille, who joined the board from Bramo. He was succeeded after the war by another Spandau man, Kurt Donath. When it became apparent that the war was lost, Hitler ordered factories to be destroyed to prevent them falling into enemy hands, but Donath, then in charge of the Munich-Milbertshofen plant, delayed carrying out the orders, realizing that there would be new masters to deal with soon.

It was hardly necessary to order the destruction of the now huge, sprawling workshops in any case. From the middle of 1941, both Milbertshofen and Spandau had been constant targets for Allied bombers, and by 1 May 1945, seven days before the final surrender, American forces took control of Munich, and the Russians had Berlin. The picture for BMW could scarcely have been more disheartening. Its pre-war car factory at Eisenach, the shadow facility at Durrehof, and the Ambi-Budd plant in Berlin which supplied BMW bodies, all fell into Russian territory and were, for all practical purposes, lost.

Milbertshofen was a bomb-scarred ruin, and Allach, although relatively unscathed, was confiscated. Not only were its factories, its workers and all

BMW made one of the most important aero-engines of the years between the wars, the BMW VI which was made under licence in the Soviet Union, and powered the first generation aircraft of the new Luftwaffe.

plans and machines lost to the East, but also a shattering blow was delivered in July 1945. The Allied Forces Control Commission declared BMW to have been an armament manufacturer, and ordered the confiscation of all facilities in the occupied zone. On 2 October, Lieutenant Colonel Eugene Keller of the American governing force demanded the complete dismantling of the Milbertshofen factory and the crating, labelling and shipment of all machines, tools and plans as a war reparation. Allach became a repair and spare parts facility for the occupying forces.

BMW ended the year with a loss of 20 million Marks. The destruction and appropriation of assets wiped a further 158 million Marks from the balance sheet. By any normal standards such a sickly entity should have shrivelled up and died – at the very least it seemed to be a powerful argument for euthanasia.

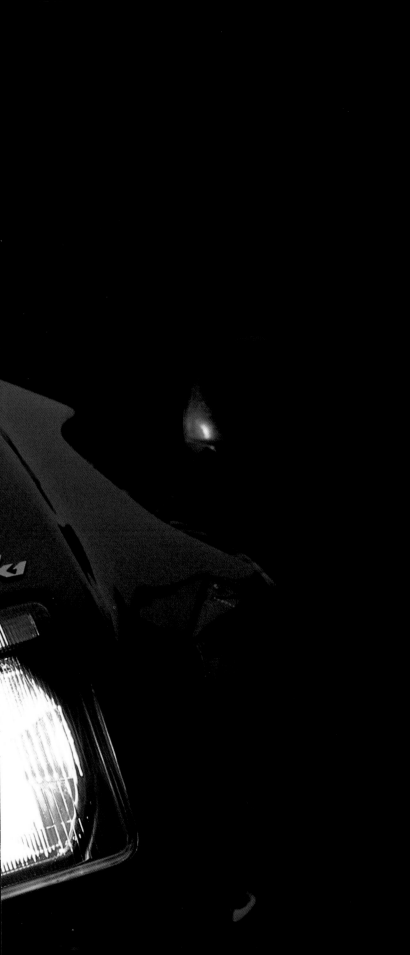

BMW's first motorcycles were primitive affairs, appearing under the unlikely name of the Flink, which means 'speedy', a quality, alas, of which they were lamentably short, and the Helios. They were the products of the Bayerische Flugzeugwerke (BFW), and were inherited by BMW following the move from Moosacher Strasse to the BFW property in Lerchenauer Strasse on 5 June 1922.

Although essentially a moped, the Flink was no lightweight, but a heavy touring bicycle with a small engine in the middle, which was started by vigorous pedalling. The two-stroke, single-cylinder, 148cc Kurier engine, designed by Curt Hanfland, then fired up, and took over the drive to the rear wheel by belt.

Once on the level, the rider could take a breather, resting his feet on the forward-mounted footboards, until he came to a hill, when he would have to pedal again to augment the meagre power of the engine.

Although the Flink, with its simple 'fore and aft' sprung forks, seems crude, it had some clever details. The single cylinder was angled forward, so that its cooling fins ran parallel with the air stream, and the magneto was bolted to the back of the crankcase at 90 degrees, to make a tidy vee with the cylinder. However, it was not a commercial success, and it is perhaps just as well that it was never sold as a BMW.

Yet BMW's engine began a great motorcycling tradition. More than other manufacturers, BMW would follow a pattern in the design of its motorcycles, carrying on the best features and

# THE

# CLASSIC

# MOTORCYCLES

The classic stance: BMW riding into the 1990s on two wheels.

relinquishing others. But rather as Emile Levassor, with his *système Panhard*, laid down the broad principles of car design in the nineteenth century (engine in front, transmitting its power through a gearbox to the back wheels), later refined by the 1901 Mercédès, so BMW followed its own critical path.

The *Bayern Kleinmotor* was a flat-twin, big enough – 493cc, with an output of 6.5bhp at 2,800rpm – to power a real motorcycle that would have no need for pedals. This was the M2B15, BMW's new universal engine, the first of the so-called boxer-motors. Designed by Martin Stolle, it was sold to Bison, SMW, SBD, and Victoria for their motorcycles. It was also used by BFW for the Helios, which came under BMW's wing after the move in 1922.

A flat-twin boxer-motor mounted across the frame would become an enduring feature of BMW motorcycles, and although the Helios had a flat-twin engine all right, the M2B15 was, perversely, mounted longitudinally, in line with the frame, with a chain drive to the rear wheel.

Like the Flink, the Helios was not a very good motorcycle. It had crude front forks, a primitive rear brake operating on a dummy belt rim, no brake at all on the front wheel and a fallible speedometer driven by a band from the front hub. Its agricultural quality was perhaps tolerated because BMW engineers were still more interested in aviation. For the time being at any rate, motorcycles represented no more than a means of generating income until they could get back to making aero engines again.

Franz-Josef Popp asked Friz to improve

The Helios motorcycle. The flat-twin engine lay fore and aft, and the drive was by chain. The classic BMW motorcycle had yet to evolve.

the Helios, which he did, but it was no longer commercially viable against the Victoria, which had acquired a more powerful engine from another manufacturer. But BMW had a large stock of Helios frames which had come with BFW in Lerchenauer Strasse, and they had to be got rid of. Friz could see the potential for growth in the motorcycle market, but without much enthusiasm, he applied himself to a machine worthy of the BMW badge, and by the time the old stock had gone, he had conceived something new.

Friz's ideas were developed by Rudolf Schleicher and Franz Bieber into a motorcycle that would become a classic. What they created was the R32, and when it was launched at the Paris Show in 1923, it astonished the industry, and established a motorcycle culture which would sustain riders for several generations to come. All the cardinal features of the most successful BMW motorcycles for the next six decades – until the arrival of the K-series in 1983 – were contained in the R32: a flat-twin engine mounted transversely; shaft drive; compliant, comfortable suspension; tubular twin triangle frame, and an elegant, well-bred appearance.

Although the R32 was not as powerful as some of its rivals, with a top speed of 60mph where others were claiming 75 or more, it was modern and reliable. It arrived on a market where many of its competitors had unreliable engines, imperfect transmissions and flimsy frames. Little wonder that it was such a success, selling at a rate of a thousand a year.

The R32's engine was similar to the M2B15 – it retained the longitudinal

A jolly weekend, *Fröliches Wochenende* is promised to readers of the Bayerische Hausfrau, provided they put on a beret and set off astride a thinly disguised Bayerische two-wheeler.

The R32. The definitive BMW motorcycle is starting to emerge, with a flat-twin engine, shaft drive, although the fins on the cylinders are still not in line with the airstream. The wooden fence separates motorcycle assembly from the rest of the works.

fins, even though it was mounted across the frame and the airflow passed round, rather than through them. With 'square' cylinder dimensions, meaning that the bore and stroke measured the same, and side-valve operation, it had a compression ratio of 5:1, and an output of 8.5bhp at 3,300rpm. The three-speed gearbox, bolted directly to the engine, had a hand-change beside the tank, and drive was through a universal joint and exposed shaft to the bevel gear housing at the back.

Motorcycle suspension was a vexing business in the early years, before hydraulic spring dampers were developed. The R32 met the problems of two-wheeler handling and roadholding with a tidy arrangement, which had a forward-facing leaf-spring, and front forks with short trailing links. Long pushrods took the springing action from the trailing links to the spring, whose bounce was kept in check by friction dampers.

There was no front brake on the first model, but for the second series a drum brake was fitted in the hub. Braking at the rear was on a dummy belt rim. The

frame was tubular, of parallel triangle design, and in all basic respects the R32 was the forerunner of the twin-cylinder motorcycles that BMW made for years to come.

It was also the forerunner of BMW racing motorcycles. In 1924 an overhead valve version of the R32 enabled Fritz Bieber to become the German National Road Racing Champion, a title won by BMW riders right through to 1932. Competition played a crucial part not only in the development of BMW machines, but also in the growth of the company's prestige in the motorcycle industry.

A sporting version of the R32, called the R37, appeared in 1925, with a more powerful overhead-valve engine developing 16bhp at 4,000rpm. It was designed by Rudolf Schleicher, as distinguished a rider as he was an engineer, for he won a gold medal with one in the 1926 British International Six Days Trial. Ten racing versions of the R37 were built, to try out tuned engines, aluminium alloy cylinder heads and improved frames – all developments which provided a useful feed-back for the design of standard production motorcycles.

Although enthusiasts tend to think of classic BMWs as principally flat-twins, single-cylinder machines were also made for forty years from 1925. It was sensible to use common components for a range of singles as well as twins. A 250cc single-cylinder appeared in 1925, the R39 with an overhead valve engine in contrast to the R32 twin which still had side valves.

First of the single-cylinder machines, the R39 had fully enclosed valve gear in a separate light-alloy head, the aluminium casting extending well up the cast-iron cylinder sleeve. Other features, such as the three-speed gearbox, trailing link front forks and drum brakes on the front wheel, were similar to the now long-running R32, but there was also a novel brake contracting on to the output shaft behind the gearbox.

Although Max Friz concentrated on the aero-engine side after 1924, the commercial success of the early BMW bikes – the production of the 25,000th was celebrated as early as 1927 – meant that motorcycles would play an essential and sometimes vital, role in BMW's success.

In 1928 the 250 and 500cc machines were supplemented by a pair of flat-twins which, although both large-capacity 750cc bikes, were quite different in character. The R62 had a side-valve engine and was primarily a touring machine, while the R63 was a sporting performer with overhead valves, and quickly joined the 500 on the track. Both racers were soon boosted by superchargers mounted above the gearbox, a means of augmenting power with which BMW engineers had been experimenting since 1926.

The result was a great improvement in out-and-out speed, but still not much sporting success. British and Italian motorcycles proved more nimble through the corners and, until the factory pulled out of circuit racing for a spell in 1930, it was mainly on the fast circuits with long straights that the Germans were successful.

Perhaps inevitably, the emphasis

gradually shifted towards outright speed records, and from 1929 Ernst Henne collected an impressive number of them on a variety of BMWs, pushing the absolute motorcycle speed record up almost every year until 1937. It was only then that the Briton Eric Fernihough retaliated, followed by the Italian Piero Taruffi. They achieved higher speeds, whereupon Henne swept along the Darmstadt *autobahn* on his totally-enclosed BMW racer to record 173.67mph (279.49kph). It was a record that would stand for fourteen years.

But although Munich could claim that a BMW was the fastest motorcycle in the world, the health of the enterprise as a whole during the depression days of the 1930s depended far more on smaller machines. During 1930, a difficult year for the industry, the R2 appeared with a 198cc single-cylinder overhead-valve engine in a lightweight frame. It was what a later generation would call a 'commuter' motorcycle, not perhaps in the BMW sporting style, but it sold in large numbers even though it was three times the price of a contemporary DKW. One advantage the class did have, however – it could be run free of Road Tax. Inside five

By 1937 Henne's record-breakers were fully faired-in streamliners. Schleicher (right, with hat) helps push him to the start on the Frankfurt Autobahn.

Tata, Hungary, 1933, and Ernst Henne straps on his streamlined helmet before attaining a speed of 244.4 km/h (152mph), to capture 21 world records in the 500cc, 750cc, and 1000cc classes.

years there were well over 15,000 buyers for R2s – it sold in greater numbers than any previous BMW machine.

Then, in 1932, the R4 was launched: a 398cc single-cylinder, which was ordered in impressive numbers by the German army. Together, these two smaller-capacity motorcycles helped the company to weather the economic collapse, which resulted in the bankruptcy of so many German industrial concerns both in the motor industry and beyond.

Big bikes were still being built, the road machines changing as the 1930s progressed, with pressed steel instead of tubular frames, heavy front mudguards, but still with the distinctive glossy black paintwork with white lining they had had since 1923. By 1935, the company's turnover was up to 128 million Reichsmarks from 19 million in 1932. With full economic stability and a series of technical innovations, Friz's conception came of age.

First, the two 750s – the side-valve R12 and the overhead-valve R17 – were fitted with telescopic front brakes incorporating hydraulic damping. This was the first time such a sophisticated and advanced suspension had been fitted to a production bike. The R12 also had a four-speed gearbox, whereas all previous BMWs had three-speed boxes. In its turn it became the most successful BMW, selling 36,000 by 1938. The sporty R17 was made in smaller numbers – about 450 in the next two years – but it had an equally important role to play in enhancing BMW's prestige.

In effect, the R17 was BMW's first

'superbike', with the (then) astonishing output of 33bhp from its very short stroke twin-carburettor engine. It was also the most powerful road machine built by BMW until the R68 model in 1952.

BMW's sporting emphasis was reinforced when the company returned to circuit racing with a flat-twin 500, using a modified form of the R17's engine. This had an overhead cam-shaft in each cylinder head, plus a supercharger on the front of the crankcase. The works team's telescopic front forks remained unique in racing, yet still BMW did not automatically start to score successes, which awaited yet another technical development. BMW handling took its greatest step forward when the factory added plunger rear suspension at the end of 1936.

Now both ends of the motorcycle were under hydraulic control, resulting in more progressive springing, better damping, and greater comfort – all developments which transferred very effectively to the bikes people bought for the road.

In 1937, BMW 500s were front runners on all the circuits of Europe and Karl Gall was the German national champion. In Britain, meanwhile, a growing market and the heart of motorcycle racing, Jock West rode a blown BMW 500 to sixth in the Senior TT on the Isle of Man, and went on to win the Ulster Grand Prix in Northern Ireland. The following year, after Karl Gall and Georg Meier were both forced out of the TT, West finished fifth, emphasizing that BMW motorcycle technology was now a match for anything in the world.

Henne's records celebrated in BMW publicity. The fastest motorcycle in the world, BMW racing successes, and a micrometer signifying BMW's commitment to accuracy were emotive images lending substance to the popular reputation of the machines.

*Following pages:* While its contemporaries often had cycle-type mudguards and slab fuel tanks strapped to the tail, the 315 had proper doors, a decent hood, and flowing lines.

Finally, in 1939, Meier became the first foreign rider ever to score a victory in the Isle of Man Senior TT – then the world's most important motorcycle race – with Jock West in second place. Sadly, their triumph was marred by the death during practice of Karl Gall, the third member of the team.

1936 was a key year for production BMWs with the launch of the R5, which had a 500cc engine with two chain-driven camshafts, one on each side of the crankshaft to keep the pushrods short. It also had a pedal-operated gearchange for the four-speed box, but because there was some doubt about how well it would work, an emergency hand lever was provided to the right of the box as well.

With the compression ratio up to 6.7:1, this flat-twin churned out 24bhp at 5,800rpm – output and peak rev figures undreamed of just a decade before. Now they had been achieved with sufficient reliability to put into produc-tion, largely thanks to a racing prog-ramme which had encouraged BMW engineers to develop their designs and try them out in the most vigorous test programme that could be devised.

A welded, rather than brazed, tubular frame made the R5 lighter and sleeker, setting the standards for all flat-twins to follow, especially when, in 1938, it was transformed into the R51 by the addition of rear suspension units with plunger telescopic spring dampers. Another technical triumph stemming directly from racing – telescopic forks and plungers were also added to the R61 and R71, 600cc and 750cc variations.

The R71, which remained available until

1941, had BMW's last side-valve boxer engine, and was popular with a sidecar market which survived well into the war years.

Small machines were also added to the range. In 1936 there was the R3, a 300cc single-cylinder machine, then the R5, a twin with a completely new version of the 494cc boxer engine used in the original R32 thirteen years earlier.

BMW motorcycles evolved rapidly in the 1930s. In Britain, AFN Ltd, already building up the car side, started importing bikes in 1935 and, even as the storm clouds gathered, still offered a full range of models, from the R23 (with 250cc ohv engine) at £59 right up to the sporty R66 (with 600cc ohv engine) at £135. They were expensive bikes – for that money you could buy a Ford Popular and still get change.

When war came, BMW stopped thinking about selling to the British and concentrated on meeting the demands of the German army. It produced huge numbers of single-cylinder machines, but the archetypal *Wehrmacht* motorcycle was the R75 flat-twin.

Unlike the *Kübelwagen* BMW produced during the war, the R75 military motorcycle, of which around 18,000 were made between 1941 and 1944, all proudly bore the Bayern roundel on their fuel tanks. In both contemporary newsreels and Hollywood's later reconstructions, this rugged combination was seen crossing the sands of the Northern Sahara for the Afrika Korps, up to its axles in mud in Northern France, or sliding over the frozen wastes of the Russian Front. The R75 became as much a part of Germany's war effort as the

Horst Mönnich's original caption to this picture in his definitive history of BMW observes that not all hands are raised. A garlanded Theo Schoth has just won the 1000cc class at the 1933 Avusrennen, and it is still early days for the Third Reich.

*Right*: By 1938, BMWs reigned supreme in the 500cc class. Only the greatest prize of the motorcycle world still eluded them — the Isle of Man TT.

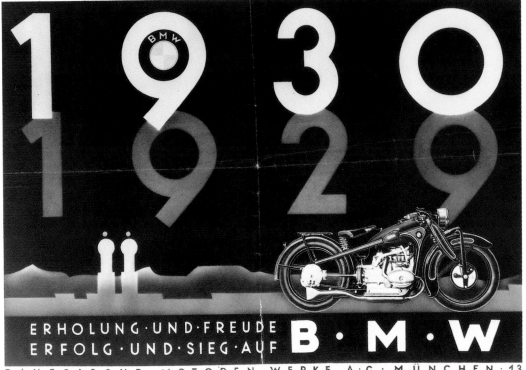

The German Jeep. One of the most versatile military transports of the Second World War, this BMW R75, with the sidecar wheel driven by a shaft, provided the Afrika Korps with traction in the deep sand of the western desert.

Focke-Wulf 190 and the Panzer Divisions. Yet it was a project from the pen of engineer, trials motorcyclist and racing driver Alex von Falkenhausen, who would continue to play a significant role in the company's development for two decades after the war as well.

Powered by a 745cc twin-cylinder engine, the R75 produced 26bhp. It looked more like a three-wheeled car with its bodywork removed, and was a complete cross-country vehicle featuring fat knobbly-treaded tyres on 16-inch wheels, with which von Falkenhausen must have been very familiar in his trials-riding days. To cope with the wide variety of conditions it would encounter, the engine fed its power through a two-stage gearbox which provided four off-road and four on-road ratios and even two reverses.

Yet the principal technical novelty was a drive to the sidecar wheel; with a lockable differential and hydraulic brakes. Good brakes were essential, not so much in view of the speed of the R75, which was little over 60mph, but in order to control its great weight, some

420kg even without three laden infantrymen and a heavy machine gun. Von Falkenhausen's wartime projects included an air/oil-cooled 2 litre military engine for use as a stationary power unit, adapting a BMW Hornet radial aero engine for fitting to a tank, and developing an engine and gearbox for a one-man tank.

By the end of the war, the main Munich factory was closed and in ruins and Eisenach, the plant where car and motorcycle production had been concentrated during the conflict to allow Munich to manufacture aircraft engines, was in the Russian sector and comandeered by the Red Army.

Only the Allach site, on the outskirts of Munich, still had some production facilities intact, and returning BMW workers began to find work there, at first servicing American forces' transport and later making cooking pots, wood planing equipment and even a few bicycles – mostly in aluminium recycled from scrap war materials, because that was all that was available.

As in 1918, the manufacture of certain items was forbidden. That included motorcycles, but by the middle of 1946 the rule was relaxed to allow small machines up to 250cc.

The man who helped re-start the motorcycle business was Georg Meier, the 1939 TT winner, who was directing plant security at the end of the war, and was on hand to get two-wheeler production up and running as soon as possible. At first, the emphasis was on the R23 250cc machines, a hundred of which were put together from spare parts. Then, at the 1948 Geneva Show, BMW unveiled the R24, a 247cc single, with a rigid, unsprung rear wheel, undamped telescopic front forks, and bolted frame construction.

It was probably just as well that the engine only gave 12 horsepower – it was not a very comfortable machine. But in post-war Germany, where every form of transport was in desperately short supply, it sold well. More than 12,000 were turned out in the next couple of years, before giving way in 1950 to the more comfortable R25, with plunger rear suspension.

That year also saw the launch of the R51/2, an updated version of the pre-war R51 flat-twin 500cc machine, with a pair of semi-downdraught carburettors mounted on the new cylinder-heads, plus an improved four-speed gearbox. Output was 24bhp, and the R51/2 combined an impressive top speed of 88mph with quality build, smooth power take-up and a steady tick-over.

Reports on the first post-war big bike were favourable, but obviously it was only a stepping-stone for BMW. Within a year, the R51/3 was launched, with

the same power output, but a considerably changed engine. It featured cooling fins on top of the rocker boxes – a style that was to continue; gear drive to the camshaft, and magneto ignition. The Bing carburettors were effectively waterproofed – a boon for all-weather riding – and there was a gearbox which, for the first time, activated a light in the headlamp shell to show when neutral had been selected. The modern era of rider-friendly machines which were easier and safer to drive was being ushered in.

Later in 1951, the first post-war BMW motorcycle of more than 500cc joined the range. The R67 was powered by a 590cc twin producing 26bhp, and was mainly designed to meet the demand for a bike with enough muscle to propel a sidecar. It was soon followed by the modified R67/2 (to go with the updated R25/2) and in 1952 re-emerged in much improved form as the sports R68, with the stunning output of 35bhp at 7,000rpm (thanks to engine tuning and higher compression heads), which meant a genuine 105mph top speed, and a far more effective twin leading shoe front brake to keep it in check.

BMW tried to follow up the success of its aero engines in the Soviet Union by selling motorcycles. Yet the publicity department felt it necessary to add CCCP to the hammer and sickle flag, as though to emphasise its intimacy with the Eastern market.

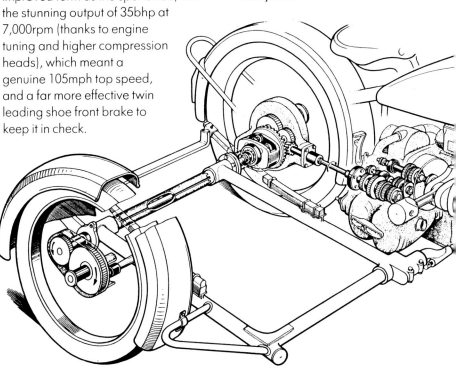

Von Falkenhausen's ingenious shaft drive, carried through the frame of the sidecar to the outrigger wheel, on the military R75.

89

It was still possible to buy a family car for the price of a BMW motorcycle, but they were selling in most cases to enthusiasts who acknowledged the quality built into BMWs, and were willing to pay for it. Export sales were steady, although not spectacular. Motorcycling was still regarded primarily as a means of transport rather than a hobby.

For a couple of years, BMW was content with minor modifications to the motorcycle range, though the R25 was again updated to R25/3 late in 1953, once again with better brakes. The demise of its predecessor, the R25/2, which had sold more than thirty-eight thousand in the previous couple of years – the most successsful BMW machine to date – coincided with the 100,000th BMW motorcycle built since the war.

On the circuits, BMW riders were faced with the task of trying to pick up from where Georg Meier had left off in 1939. In the early post-war years, German factories and riders were restricted to local events, and when they were re-admitted to Fédération Internationale Motocycliste (FIM) competition in 1951, Meier and the young Walter Zeller were not very successful. The

The R50 of 1955 startled the world of motorcycling with Earles-type front forks in which the hub was carried on forward-facing arms pivoting on the steering frame. Swinging-arm suspension at the rear made the BMW one of the most comfortable road bikes of the day.

BMW Rennsport racing twin was not yet sufficiently developed.

Later in the 1950s, the solo machines had to compete against highly sophisticated Italian Gileras, MVs and Guzzis ridden by John Surtees and Geoff Duke. Even so, Walter Zeller finished second to Surtees in the 1956 world championship, but it was the nearest a BMW solo rider came to glory in the fierce chase for the title.

Sidecar racing was more promising, especially during the 1954 season, when Willie Noll's BMW became a serious threat to the domination of the British world champion Eric Oliver on his Norton. Oliver won most of the races in the early part of the year, and managed to slip past Noll near the end of a hectic event at the Nürburgring; Noll won the last three races of the season to take the title, beginning a record run of nineteen world championships between 1954 and 1974.

At the end of 1954 Willie Noll broke an impressive number of records at the Montlhéry circuit near Paris, on a fully streamlined BMW sidecar record-breaker. From ten miles up to a hundred miles and finally the one-hour duration, Noll's combination set new marks at between 106 and 114mph.

Yet that was nothing to what he achieved the next year, in a bizarre machine that looked like something between a motorcycle and a small aeroplane. With a high tail and Plexiglas canopy, it had a strutted wheel off to one side forming the 'sidecar'. Powered by an unblown but fuel-injected 500, said to reach 10,000rpm, this amazing contraption

In the early 1950s, BMW was overwhelmed in world championship road racing by MV, Mondial, Guzzi, Norton, Gilera, and AJS. Even DKW and NSU got a look in, but BMW publicity made the most of what victories it did score.

recorded 174mph over a flying mile on the Munich-Ingolstadt *autobahn*.

BMW had already created a stir in 1955, by launching two new models at the Brussels Show. They were the 500cc R50 and the 600cc R69. Both featured Earles-type front forks, which had the spring-damper units working on two leading links pivoting on a mounting behind the mudguard, and full swinging arm rear suspension – developments once again proven on the company's racing bikes. The rear suspension pre-load meant that the damper rate could be varied by a simple lever when a pillion passenger was carried and, for the first time, the drive shaft was enclosed within the right leg of the swinging arm. The 35bhp R69 had a top speed of over 100mph, and was a fast and luxurious machine, even if, at £500 in Britain, it was by no means cheap.

Gradually, however, the motorcycle market was running out of steam. Scooters were all the rage, and big bikes like BMWs looked expensive to buy and run. Production slumped badly in 1956 – at 15,500 barely half what it had been in 1955 – and by the time of the Frankfurt Show that autumn, BMW had stopped building motorcycles because stocks were so high.

The Suez Crisis of November 1956 cast its shadow over the market, the resulting oil shortage in Europe distorting the market for some years. Reflecting the slump in demand for expensive, thirsty cars, the motorcycle market also went for fuel-efficient smaller machines.

The following year was even worse; just 5,400 machines were built, so there were no new models for 1958 and

Bonnet straps and cowled headlights, the BMW 328, the antithesis of sports cars which hitherto had hard springs and a flexible chassis. Soft springs and a stiff frame produced better results.

1959. No fresh two-wheelers emerged from BMW until September 1960, and the next Frankfurt Show, and even that was only the result of the corporate rescue plan devised at the end of 1959, which called urgently for new models to revive sales.

The campaign was begun with a new 250cc machine, the R27. The flat-twins and the sports R50 and R69 were provided with more power, each with an 'S' added to the designation. In bike parlance, '50' or '60' was shorthand for the engine capacity, 500cc, or 600cc. It was a useful means of identification but, like the system used for the cars, had its own anomalies. In the case of the R69, the '9' simply represents the ninth of a series of changes to the 600.

The R27 proved to be the last single-cylinder motorcycle BMW made, and it was manufactured right through to 1967. With output up to 18bhp at 7,400rpm, and the engine assembly and exhaust on rubber mountings, it was a lively and refined machine. The R50S and R96S now had 35bhp for the 500 and 42 for the 600 – and that meant top speeds of 100 and 110mph respectively. Hydraulic steering dampers and vibration dampers on the engine improved the ride and refinement, and the factory was able to claim, quite truthfully, that the R69S was the fastest motorcycle made in Germany.

The range settled down for the 1960s, maintaining its traditional values and style, while the market changed around it. Quality machines in general found fewer buyers, and a flood of models from Japan more or less destroyed the British industry. BMW dropped the R50S – most sporting bikers who could afford

a BMW preferred the R69S anyway. There was a sudden vogue for motorcycling in the United States, and US-market-only models were quickly launched to exploit it. These had telescopic forks rather than the Earles-type of the European machines, plus – of course – higher and wider handlebars.

BMW persevered with this range through a thin market, surviving into the 1960s thanks largely to the revised fortunes of the car side, following the introduction of the 1500 in 1961. It was just as well that the cars were making a profit, because for the best part of the decade there was precious little gained from the motorcycles. Matters did not improve until the 'Stroke 5' machines appeared in 1969, by which time motorcycle production had moved to the Spandau factory in Berlin.

Three new machines were based on common frames and many similarities within the engines, which were of 500, 600 and 750cc capacity. All were traditional BMW flat-twins, with unitary gearboxes and shaft drive. The frames were much lighter than before (BMWs had been putting on weight in the 1960s); front suspension was by telescopics with plenty of travel to soak up the bumps; the electrics were 12 volt, and the two bigger machines had the luxury of electric starters.

Now, at last, buyers were offered alternative colours. Black with white lining had been almost the only choice available (white with black lining had been tried out but was not popular). Now the 500 and 750 Stroke 5s could be bought with silver mudguards and tanks, and soon there were other colours as well. BMWs even appeared with chrome-plated panels on the tank sides – an event perhaps not unconnected with the appointment of Bob Lutz, the American motorcycling enthusiast regarded as something of a motor industry phenomenon, as Sales Director. The flashy panels were not popular, however, and soon disappeared – together with Lutz to Ford and later Chrysler.

The Stroke 5 motorcycles were produced with only minor changes until the end of 1973, some even selling in Britain, despite deterrent prices. The 1970 sales tickets were £763 for the R50/5, £826 for the R60/5, and £999 for the R75/5.

Late in 1973, the Stroke 5s became the Stroke 6s, with four machines based closely on their predecessors. The 500cc model was dropped, and the range was shifted upward by the addition of two 900cc superbikes. Other major changes were that disc brakes were standard on all but the R60/6, and a five-speed gearbox now became common for all. Headlamps, instruments and controls were also modified to complete an overall appearance which was to continue into the late 1980s.

The two flagship models, the R90/6 and the R90S, looked more dramatic than ever. An exemplary finish, especially to the mechanical parts, was always a characteristic of BMWs. Cylinder and crankcase castings were invariably smooth, and crisply sculpted; paintwork was faultless, and during the post-war period, when competitive bikes from Japan were appearing in eye-catching colours, with a similarly high standard of finish, BMW designers spared no effort to maintain theirs.

Now, they tackled their rivals head-on and for the first time employed a stylist, Hans Muth. He gave the sporty R90S a dual seat, a fairing cowl, and a shimmering airbrush paint job on the tank, seat and fairing. With 67bhp at 7,000rpm, and twin disc brakes on the front wheel, it was also a sparkling performer, capable of a 0–60mph time of about 4.5 seconds and a top speed of 120mph. Detail improvements throughout the range came in 1975, including the use of perforated discs for the brakes and – after all these years – the final elimination of the kick start, although it remained available as a option.

In 1976 the Cologne Show saw the launch of the Stroke 7 series, with yet another shift upwards – the models were now 600cc, 750cc and 1000cc. But the most significant development in view of the trend towards modern, streamlined motorcycles, influenced by those used in racing, and the new Japanese models, was that the R100 could be bought with full fairings as the R100RS. A great deal of work had been done in the Pininfarina wind tunnel in Italy to contrive a fairing that not only

Larger, more colourful BMWs competed for style with the new Japanese machines, but their quality was unwavering.

provided a pocket of still air around the rider, but also applied downthrust on the front wheel for stability at speed. The R100RS was a superb new concept in speedy touring motorcycles, but the price of £2,899 was daunting, at a time when superbikes from Honda, Benelli, Guzzi and Ducati were all under £2,000.

The R100RS could do 116mph and a contemporary road-test achieved over 47mpg. 'You can cruise the R100RS at 100mph all day without being buffeted by a hurricane,' testers wrote ecstatically.

Police forces all over the world were choosing BMWs for their reliability, and British forces were using the new ones with fairings. As with cars, sales to the police were important to the marketing strategy of the British subsidiary of BMW. In 1976, fifty modified machines were on duty with various forces; by May 1978 the figure had increased to a thousand; in 1980 the two thousandth BMW machine for police use in Britain arrived on the Press Day of the London Motor Cycle Show; and by the 1980s, almost every force in Britain was using them.

Yet, in the early years of the decade, the Motorcycle Division had been struggling. It was competing with sophisticated – and reliable – rivals from Japan at the same time as contending with powerful, if quality-flawed, sports machines from Italy. Sales in the important American market suffered because of the strength of the German currency against the dollar.

One answer was to widen the range. At the top end various refinements were incorporated into the big twins, including cast alloy wheels and

changes to controls and instrumentation. The R100RT was added, intended to be the ultimate touring machine. It had a fuller fairing than the RS, and panniers were added for the growing number of riders who used their bikes for serious touring. Weighty enough unladen, it became rather ponderous when fully loaded, and proved curiously popular with older riders.

The more obvious expansion was at the bottom end of the range. In an attempt to compensate for sales lost by dropping the 500cc and 600cc twins, and the elevation of the 750 into an 800cc as the R80/7, two smaller-capacity motorcycles, the R45 and the R65, were introduced. The R45, BMW's smallest-ever flat-twin, produced a mere 35bhp and struggled to reach a top speed of 99mph. It was not a success. The R65 was little more muscular, but its maximum of 108mph was disappointing compared with some of the competition – especially as the middleweight BMWs were not much cheaper than the big twins.

In 1980, one more big twin joined the range, this time with very sporting overtones. It was the R80G/S trail bike, designed to exploit the company's success in various long-distance events, the International Six Days Trial and the most gruelling test of all, the Paris-Dakar Rally.

Developed in collaboration with the Italian manufacturer Laverda, the RS80G/S ('G' for 'gelände' or 'country') was intended as a trials-style road bike rather than a genuine off-roader. It pioneered monolever rear suspension within the BMW range – known under the BMW patent as Paralever – which

The K1, one of the most aerodynamically correct motorcycles ever, wind-tunnel-tested to provide the rider with an envelope of calm Sculpted fairings, smooth power, sports car comfort, the epitome of the modern sports-touring motorcycle.

dispensed with two arms for carrying the rear wheel, replacing them with one, which allowed greater suspension travel. The off-roader had a 797cc engine developing 49bhp, which gave it a top speed of 107mph. Certainly its lighter weight and long-travel suspension captured the enthusiasm of contemporary testers. One motorcycle weekly declared the R80G/S BMW best roadster 'and the most memorable machine of the year.'

A special rally held early in 1983 was supposed to be celebrating sixty years of BMW motorcyles. But, as industry insiders already knew, it really commemorated sixty years of flat-twin engined BMW motorcycles, for just three months later came the K-series, a totally new generation of BMWs.

Instead of the flat-twin, air-cooled boxer-motors, they had in-line, water-cooled fours. Nothing like it had happened since Volkswagen and Porsche forsook flat, air-cooled boxer-motors mounted at the rear, and changed to upright, water-cooled four-cylinder engines at the front – in VW's case driving the front wheels. Like Porsche, BMW was determined to keep its traditional designs going alongside the new.

But even though it was effectively the start of a new epoch for BMW bikes, the launch of the K-series BMWs occasioned little surprise. Four-cylinder BMW engines had been rumoured as early as the winter of 1978, and in 1981 the company confirmed that it was tooling up for the production of a new

The Paris-Daker established a new class of off-road sporting motorcycle, tough, fast and worthy of the generic title *Enduro*.

1 litre water-cooled four, and had set aside £35.3 million to double motorcycle production by the mid-1980s. So when the K100 was unveiled in October 1983, there was an eager audience waiting.

The speculation before the launch centred around the disposition of the engine. Would BMW put it across the frame, Japanese-style? That would lose the flat-twin's advantage of a low centre of gravity, while also making shaft drive to the rear wheel difficult. If the crankshaft lay across the frame, the drive would have to turn through a right angle to reach the rear wheel by shaft. Japanese transverse 'fours' did not have the same problem, since they continued to drive by chains, but, for BMW, such a solution would have been unthinkable.

The answer was a brilliant piece of engineering – the Compact Drive System. The engine was laid on its side, so the weight could be kept low, and the crankshaft was aligned on the central axis of the machine. The whole system formed an integral part of the chassis.

The engine was an all-light-alloy double overhead camshaft unit, water-cooled and fuel-injected, of 987cc capacity and developing 90bhp. It would power the K100 to a maximum of 126mph, while providing plenty of torque in the mid-speed ranges to make it a most tractable and refined machine. Rear suspension was by Paralever, R80G/S style, and braking by three large perforated discs, two in front and one behind. Launched in Britain at £3,290, it looked inexpensive by BMW standards.

There were some reservations among testers, who withheld their praise until the K100RS appeared a few months later, complete with a sports fairing and an extra £1,000 on the price. The extra plastic in front made the K100 into a quiet and comfortable long-distance cruiser. Then, for those who wanted more substantial protection against the elements, the K100RT followed, with full fairing and panniers.

It was already known that a three-cylinder, 750cc version of the K was in the course of preparation, and it came along in 1985, quickly attracting a devoted clientele, for it proved to have a smoother-spinning engine than the larger model, together with more nimble handling.

One tester achieved 124mph from the K75C, while another rode from the

North Cape of Norway to the South of France, averaging over 58mpg and using just half a pint of oil.

The K1, pinnacle of BMW's four-cylinder development, was launched at the Cologne Show at the end of 1988, celebrating the production of the 100,000th K-series machine. It was designed to meet formidable competition from high-performance sports machines produced by the Japanese following their experience in motorcycle Grand Prix racing. The K1 combined superb lines with advanced technical developments, to be the most spectacular BMW two-wheeler ever. Enthusiasts – particularly in Germany, where it went on sale at the end of May 1989 – clamoured to place orders, showing that BMW had once again caught the mood of the buyers.

To go with the wind-cheating body panels and wheel covers, the K1 also had a reinforced frame, new-style light alloy wheels and modified suspension. The engine featured four valves per cylinder for the first time, which, with a higher compression ratio, provided 100bhp at 8,000rpm. It could have been higher, but the company was anxious not to get into a 'power battle' and kept the K1 engine to a limit of 100bhp to improve the more useful torque – 100Nm at 6,750rpm.

Nevertheless, the K1 proved spectacularly fast. It would reach 60mph from rest in well under four seconds, and go on to 143mph. Controlling performance like this needed bigger brake discs front and rear, and the option of the first effective motorcycle anti-lock system, as pioneered by BMW on the K-series in the spring of 1988.

But the K1, like its four-wheeled counterparts the M3, M5 and Z1, was not planned for manufacture in large numbers. It was limited to 4,000 units in the whole of 1989, making it likely that, with demand exceeding supply, this sleekest and swiftest of all BMW motorcycles would become something of a collector's item.

With the arrival of the K1, fairing and specification variations on both the K100 and the K75, plus the continuing R65, R80, R80G/S and their derivatives, BMW had well over a dozen models by the end of the 1980s. The company may well have given up any thought of being competitive with solo machines on the race circuits, but they could still aspire with some confidence to capture the enthusiasm and admiration of those motorcyclists who recognized an understated appearance, apt design and careful manufacture.

Sculpted fairings, smooth power, sports car comfort, the epitome of the modern sports-touring motorcycle.

It was more than three years before BMWs wounds healed sufficiently to allow the production of its first post-war motorcycle. It was over seven years before the first car. Yet it was something of a miracle that it happened at all.

All that remained in those desolate years of Germany's recovery was BMW's design philosophy. It survived in the machine tools, plans, patterns and stocks that had been distributed all over the world as reparations. But until such time as conditions would allow the famous name to be applied to what BMW was always best at – making engines – keeping the name alive had to be left to outside agencies.

Although little consolation at the time, it was a tribute to BMW's engineering reputation that this philosophy was thought worth preserving. Reincarnations of the great BMWs of the 1930s, some good, others less good, proved of value in keeping the name alive, and, every bit as important, BMW and BMW-derived cars still managed to score successes in motor sport. The investment in the sports cars of the 1930s, and in that great six-cylinder engine of Fiedler and Schleicher, paid off in the 1940s, by continually reminding enthusiasts – drivers whose memories of the Bayerische Motoren had to span ten years – of the cars that had left their mark on motoring history.

As BMW workers in Munich salvaged what little they could, across the border in the newly-created Deutsche Demokratische Republik, Wartburg Castle overlooked the fourth owners of the Eisenach factory. The Soviet Autovelo concern was charged with

# ALTERNATIVE
## BMWs
KEEPING

THE NAME

ALIVE

Wheel spats, a small back window, deeply swaged curves, and a spare wheel under a separate cover, European styling in the 1930s was already going America's way. The dummy knock-off wheel nuts, a feature of the car when new, are something of an affectation however.

The ruins of 1945. Radial piston aero engines and in the background a wrecked jet lie among the wreckage of the BMW factory at the end of the war.

plant was in place to make them, with the old designs much of the old workforce. None of these had ever been in Munich, yet there was a certain amount of discomfiture in Bavaria about the treasured blue and white quartered symbol appearing on cars that were manifestly not being made by BMW.

The precious trademark was too valuable to be used indiscriminately. It was one of the few assets of which BMW could not be stripped, and Munich was determined to ensure that it remained the property of the Bavarian component of the firm. Eisenach was not after all in Bavaria. Munich was where BMW had been founded, and Eisenach had only come under the wing of BMW by historical accident.

To remedy the situation, BMW formally disowned the Eisenach plant in the autumn of 1949, twenty-one years after acquiring it as the Dixi factory. A successful legal action was fought, and the disputed badge was removed from the eastern imposters. It was replaced by a similar design quartered in red and white, and the company took the name of the Eisenacher Motoren Werke (EMW). Importers with stocks of the offending cars in Western Europe were obliged to file the sides of the 'B' on both the external badge and on the one cast on the engine block to make an 'E', and paint the blue portions of the badges red.

EMW 321s were made in quite large numbers. Around 10,000 were turned out between 1945 and 1950, almost three times as many as BMW made before the war. Eisenach also made a number of 327s, with some curious modifications such as hinging the doors

dismantling BMW's car plant. Fortunately the zealous Russians, who as a rule took things to pieces on their side of the new frontier faster than the Americans in the West, quickly recognized its commercial potential. Eisenach workers had assembled some BMW 321s from left-over spares, while Autovelo brought in presses from Ambi-Budd's Berlin factory, which had built BMW bodies before the war.

By the end of 1945, 68 spare-part BMW 321s had been produced with the old 45bhp engine. The following year 1,373 were made, and in 1947 a further 2,000. These counterfeit BMWs were not available to the general public; they were used instead by the new military regime, and its nominees, doctors and party functionaries, but they were also actively exported. Much-needed foreign currency was earned for the nascent state, and concessionaires were appointed in Switzerland, the Low Countries, Denmark and Sweden.

These eastern BMWs were much the same as the pre-war cars. All the old

from the rear instead of the front which was safer, and different hubcaps, instruments and hood detailing. It had the 55 horsepower engine, but otherwise it was little changed, and over 500 were made between 1949 and 1955.

BMW was relieved when its precious badge disappeared from EMWs and equally pleased when the 321 ceased production in 1950. Poor materials and indifferent quality control resulted in cars that did nothing for BMW's reputation. The 321 was replaced by the BMW-EMW 340 which was, in effect, a 326 chassis with a new body featuring a broad triangular grille with tranverse bars, removing the visual association with the old firm. With a twin-carburettor 55bhp engine the 340 bore little resemblance to a BMW, particularly the drab, strictly utilitarian ambulance and wooden-sided shooting-brake.

Before Autovelo handed Eisenach back to the East German government as an operational nationalized industry, it had developed the 342 and 343 limousines. One had a traditional BMW kidney grille, and the other was designed to appeal to American tastes. Neither reached production, nor did the 340S, a lightweight two-seater roadster based on BMW 328 mechanicals. EMW took them seriously enough to exhibit them at motor shows, but in a centrally planned economy such quality as remained in them was bound to take second place, in the long run, to quantity.

The BMW lineage at Eisenach died with the 327 and 340 in 1955. The Wartburg identity was resurrected for a three-cylinder, two-stroke economy car which

popped and banged its way through the 1960s in a haze of oily smoke that came to be characteristic not only of the cities of Eastern Europe, but also of those tourists who ventured out into the West.

Before consigning Eisenach to history, however, the engineers at the Thuringian factory made one further contribution to the story of BMW. They established the EMW *Rennkollectiv*, or racing team, and entered East German races during the early 1950s with highly streamlined two-seat sports cars based on the 328. Occasional incursions into West Germany at the Avus, Solitude and Nürburgring circuits showed that they were very competitive.

Later known as AWE (Automobil Werke Eisenach), the team made a number of appearances outside Germany, when the cars were driven by Edgar Barth, later a European hill-climb champion, and Arthur Rosenhammer. They even won a race at Montlhéry, and with the highly modified twin overhead

Using as many of the old body-pressings as possible, the Eisenach factory in East Germany tried to disguise the BMW origins of the post-war product. Quality was poor and BMW successfully disputed the use of the name and the badge.

camshaft engine producing at least 135bhp, Barth actually beat Stirling Moss in a Cooper-Alta in the 1953 Eifelrennen at the Nürburgring. This line of development unfortunately came to a halt when the factory went over to the disagreeable two-stroke in 1955, although the team did race occasionally in 1956.

Meanwhile, in West Germany, enthusiasm for motor racing was as keen as ever. A certain perseverance was needed to take part in motor sporting events in those dark years. Europe had little fuel, few tyres, and specialist metals were almost unobtainable. Such materials as were available had to be directed towards the reconstruction of homes and industry for both victors and vanquished. Motor racing could hardly stake much of a claim against such competition.

The sport recovered slowly, first with old cars, then with modified versions of them – a different kind of spring here and a new cylinder head there. Pre-war cars reappeared from storage, were rebuilt, carefully prepared, and then raced much as they had been six, seven and eight years before. Predictably the same ones proved successful, and the 328 was a firm favourite.

The French were the first to organize a race, appropriately enough in view of the headquarters of motor racing being the offices of the Automobile Club de France, in the Place de la Concorde in Paris. It was a low-key affair, run in the Bois de Boulogne in September 1945.

In many of the races that followed in Belgium, Britain, Italy and Switzerland, the 328 carried the BMW colours.

Autenrieth Coachbuilders of Darmstadt made the bodywork for both the Coupé and this Cabriolet version of the 327. The completed bodies were transported to the factory at Eisenach which housed BMW's entire car production up till 1939.

One of the fathers of the modern BMW, Freiherr (Baron) Alex von Falkenhausen.

British drivers such as Leslie Johnson, Tony Crook and Betty Haig raced theirs at home and abroad, and the young Stirling Moss entered his first competitive events in his father's BMW during 1947. French and Belgian drivers used 328s to revive racing, but it was not long before events overtook the veteran design.

Country by country, new kinds of racing emerged, and new cars came out, together with new racing formulae in tune with the times. In Formula B, as it was known before it came to be called Formula 2; HWM, Alta and Connaught came to the fore. Jaguar, Frazer Nash, Cooper, and a host of small, specialized constructors built new sports cars, and single-seaters for the new 500cc racing class. France had Talbot and Gordini, while Italian drivers could choose from Maserati, Alfa Romeo, OSCA, Cisitalia and a new name, Ferrari. Under those circumstances it was quite natural that the main thrust of post-war development for the venerable 328 was left to Germany.

Organizing motor sporting events in Germany was still, at the very least, problematical. Official permission had to be obtained to move from one zone of the country to another, and owing to the food shortages, entry forms stipulated that drivers had to bring their own bread. Lavish 'hospitality suites' at motor races lay a long way in the future.

Nevertheless, a hill-climb event took place as early as 1946, at Ruhestein in the Black Forest, and it was won outright by the 1940 Mille Miglia car, the Touring-built coupé loaned for the occasion to Hermann Lang, who beat

Alex von Falkenhausen's normal 328. In 1947, Karl Kling drove the Kamm-inspired Mille Miglia car to victory in the first post-war circuit race at Hockenheim. This car now belonged to Ernst Loof, who had managed the BMW team effort at Brescia in 1940, and who now proved to be a key member of the German racing revival.

Loof, Georg Meier (the 1939 Senior TT victor) and Lorenz Dietrich had met during the war in Paris, where they determined to develop a new German racing car as soon as hostilities ceased. They wasted little time and, in March 1947, formed BMW-Veritas (Latin for truth) at Hausern. Under Allied occupation rules they were forbidden to build engines of more than 1 litre, but they were allowed to rebuild old engines.

Veritas attracted enthusiasts who wanted their old 327 or 328 to go faster, so with his Mille Miglia experience Loof was able to put new life into now ageing BMWs. He also knew enough to develop lightweight and highly aerodynamic aluminium bodies for the two-seater Veritas 'Rennsports'. Although the slab-sided RS was no beauty, its functional design was worthy of the German 'Silver Arrow' tradition, and the combination of a 125bhp engine and a light, torsionally stiff body enabled the Veritas RS to reach 135mph.

Veritas cars appeared in increasing numbers, and won the German 2 litre sports car championship in 1947, 1948 and 1949, adding the 1½ litre class in 1949 by short-stroking the 328 engine. Loof became ambitious, and contested a growing number of F2 events with a single-seater. German drivers were not allowed to race in international events until 1950, but the speed of the slippery Veritas on fast circuits such as the Grenzlandring and Avus brought enquiries from abroad.

The cars also performed well against more sophisticated opposition abroad, often as 'Meteors' since there was still prejudice against driving a German car. Veritas won at Montlhéry, Chimay and on many German circuits, but by 1949 it was apparent that a new engine was needed to maintain a competitive edge.

Accordingly, Loof developed one, with a single overhead camshaft, which he had made for Veritas by Heinkel, the aeroplane manufacturer. Traces of its BMW ancestry remained, and the Heinkel unit produced 140bhp at 6,500rpm and a predicted top speed of 150mph. Lack of development prevented a serious challenge to Ferrari and Gordini, but some cars were equipped with bubble-top canopies to extract the last ounce of speed, and the Veritas still had no real opposition within Germany.

Nearly fifty Veritas racing cars were built, and they were seen on starting grids well into the 1950s. Although it had limited success internationally, Veritas became well known in Germany, much as Lotus did in Britain as a result of its success in local club racing a decade later.

The parallel with Lotus is all the more appropriate since Veritas (very quickly obliged to drop the BMW prefix) fostered the idea of building road-going cars. Following a cosmological theme, they offered the Comet Coupé sports car, the Saturn Coupé and the

Scorpion Convertible in 1949 and 1950. A five- or six-seater Jupiter saloon was planned to complete the heavenly host, but it was never built. Such ambitious schemes in the austere times amounted to very little, however, and only sixteen cars were ever completed, despite encouraging press reviews. They were expensive, and Germany did not have enough rich buyers in 1950.

The partnership split in 1950, Dietrich setting up a new factory in Muggersturm to produce the Dyna-Veritas, based on Panhard components. This was a light and pretty two- and four-seat car which was more appropriate for the times. Around 155 were produced in 1951 and 1952, before undercapitalization and lack of bank support led to the inevitable collapse in 1952. Despite this, Loof tried to re-establish Veritas at the Nürburgring. A typically ambitious programme announcing six new luxury Veritas-Nürburgring models met with only twenty orders, and Loof was forced to close the doors of Veritas for ever. Before he left the Eifel district, however, he produced his version of the forthcoming BMW 507, which was considered and rejected by the works.

The long wheelbase version of the Veritas Coupé. The make enjoyed a good run of success on the race track, but attempts to produce a series of road cars proved fruitless.

With ingenious independent springing, four wheel drive, and a stout sheet metal floor-pan, the BMW 325 was extremely advanced for 1937. It was also made by Stoewer in Stettin and Hanomag in Hanover; BMW avoided using its famous quartered emblem on this model.

He returned to the company, which had re-started production of real BMWs, and died in 1956.

During the war von Falkenhausen's home was damaged by Allied bombing, but his beloved 328 remained intact. He removed the wheels at the beginning of the war, and even after the fall of the Third Reich, hid them to save the car from the depredations of American servicemen; without wheels they would be less likely to purloin it. Now he could bring it out for the Ruhestein hill-climb, and start it off on a career which would play an increasingly important part in his life for several years.

Von Falkenhausen's situation, was however, not easy. 'I had no job. What should I do? It seemed better to do what I really liked, so I decided to build cars. I had some 328 engines, but it was difficult to get new materials. Fuel could be obtained from the US forces in exchange for Schnapps, and I had a friend with access to an ex-military factory which belonged now to nobody. It was filled with coal and

alcohols, so with a little money I could brew racing fuels.'

Encouraged by some good results in 1946, von Falkenhausen fitted the engine from his trusty 328 (chassis number 85336) into his first *Eigenbau*, or special. It was named ALFA-BMW (after ALex von Falkenhausen, later AFM for Alex von Falkenhausen Munich), and his 1947 diary records the engine as having an 11.3:1 compression ratio running on a rich mixture of 33% Benzin, 33% Benzole, 18% Methyl Alcohol and 15% Methyl Acetone.

He ran both 1.5 and 2.0 litre cars, the 1.5 derived from his 315/1 engine, with a 328 head. Even before the war he had raised its power from 45bhp to 78bhp at 6,000rpm, and continued with development to clinch the 1½ litre German sports car championship in 1947 and 1948. This first *Eigenbau* used BMW 326 torsion bar rear suspension with a 328 chasis.

Von Falkenhausen could have gone down the Veritas route, and built racing cars for sporting clients, with a production equivalent road car for sale, but lack of capital forced him to concentrate on only one side of the business, and he chose racing. 'Veritas had more money and more people,' he said. 'I had no money at all.'

He did build a weird-looking streamlined car for one customer, Emil Vorster, with an 1100cc Fiat engine which had a special three-valve head (one inlet, two exhaust) cast by BMW. 'They were happy to get an order.' Yet for the most part the factory was not much help, making the wheels for von Falkenhausen's single-seater, but

Successive BMWs manage to retain their identity. Fifteen years and an entire generation of automotive style and design separate the 327 and the 502, but the lineage is plain to see.

surprisingly little else. 'They were desperate for any work just to keep the factory going. They once sold me a 328 cylinder head for half price, but told me not to come back, it was the only one I would get.'

Von Falkenhausen only made seven AFM racing cars, but they achieved a reputation that belied their numbers. Starting with the stripped 328, he made 1½ and 2 litre versions, but it was the single-seater built in 1949 that secured AFM's place in history. Sporting a light tubular frame, independent suspension, a de Dion rear axle with torsion bars and alloy wheels, it weighed just 420kg, exactly the same as the military motorcycle Falkenhausen designed for BMW with just 26bhp.

Compared with 500kgs for a Veritas and rather more for a Ferrari, the AFM offered a significant power-to-weight advantage. Von Falkenhausen's other advantage was that he had an Austrian driver, Hans Stuck Senior, who by virtue of his nationality was permitted to race in international events.

Stuck, who drove for Auto Union pre-war, was an acknowledged *bergmeister*, mountain champion, and won the hill-climbs at Maloja and Freiburg with the AFM single-seater. Even though he was probably past his best, Stuck and the AFM could put up invigorating performances so long as the car held together. On one occasion in 1949, he led the entire Ferrari team, with Fangio, Ascari and Villoresi, on their home ground at Monza – until the engine expired.

On that occasion it was bearing trouble, a frequent problem at a time when good bearings were hard to find.

Nevertheless it proved that a thirteen-year-old production-derived engine was still capable of a good performance against a modern racing 12-cylinder. However, it was also an important occasion in another way. It was a watershed for German self-respect in a sport in which they had once been almost unbeatable. It showed they still had the capacity to repeat the accomplishment.

Stuck repeated his Monza form the following year, in the Grand Prix of the Autodrome, Monza on 28 May 1950, when he won heat 2 (eight laps, about 32 miles) at 101.2mph, 0.8 sec ahead of Ascari (Ferrari). Ferraris took the first five places in the final, with Villoresi, Ascari, Serafini, Tadini and Bianchetti. Villoresi won at an average speed of 101.5mph and set the fastest lap at 104.16mph. The AFM retired in the final, but the Italians had been shown that German technology and enterprise were not entirely crushed.

The Italians won more or less as they pleased for the rest of the season, but it was important to know that the car had at least the legs of the opposition. The 328 engine was growing old, however, and, like his competitors at Veritas, von Falkenhausen needed to replace it. Unlike the Loof-Heinkel engine, AFM's 2 litre V8 bore no relationship to its BMW predecessor, but it lived only to share the fate of the Veritas since there was not enough money to carry out development.

Although it was fast, the *Küchen* engine, as it was known, rarely lasted the pace, and was eventually replaced by a Bristol. AFMs continued to appear in German events until 1953, when they gradually disappeared from view, only a couple of museum pieces surviving. Yet the experience von Falkenhausen gained was invaluable. He was recalled to BMW, where his engineering and organizational skills were put to work, and the AFM became another piece in the mosaic of BMW's post-war recovery.

Other hopeful racers also used BMW components – the pretty HH48 of Hermann Holbein and the rear-engined Polensky, for example – but they had little success. The 500cc and 750cc motorcycle engines enjoyed a short lease of life in Germany's version of the popular 'half-litre' racing class. Yet, despite these lively developments in German motor sport, the most significant and lasting development for the 328 engine took place in Britain.

The Aldington brothers and their AFN company had not only enjoyed good business importing BMWs and calling them Frazer Nash-BMWs before the war, but they had also developed close personal links with BMW directors and engineers. H. J. Aldington flew to Munich soon after the end of hostilities, ostensibly to reclaim his 328, which had been crashed at Hamburg in 1939. Having visited many of his friends, he came away not with his old car, but one of the Mille Miglia sports cars, which he promptly drove back to England.

AFN had been trying to secure its future. Aldington had concluded that his former principal supplier would not be able to deliver cars for some time, so he had to look round for an alternative. When he learned that the Bristol Aeroplane Company was thinking of making cars to replace the aircraft production they would undoubtedly lose as the war finished, he showed

Alex von Falkenhausen racing his first AFM, based on a pre-war 328, in a 1947 race at Hockenheim.

them his BMW 327. It was just the sort of car Bristol had been looking for, so, with the same eye to the future as the Aldingtons, Bristol bought a majority shareholding in AFN.

As an established manufacturer of aero engines, it was easy for Bristol to obtain official permission to visit Munich where, ostensibly, engineers could inspect a high-altitude test facility at BMW. H. J. and Don Aldington joined the team, and while they were there, the Stirling bomber which had been pressed into service to take them was loaded with technical drawings and details of the 326, 327 and 328 BMWs. They also brought back two engines, a 318, 1.8 litre twin-cam prototype, and a 335, 3½ litre.

The Aldingtons wanted to develop the 3½ litre, but Bristol decided firmly on the 2 litre. The plans were taken officially as a war reparation, and Fritz Fiedler, the BMW Engineering Director, also came to Bristol as a 'reparation', at H. J. Aldington's request.

A BMW engine incorporating some of

Bristol's metallurgical experience was tested in May 1946 and fitted to a BMW 327/8 for road testing. When the Bristol 400 was revealed at the 1947 Geneva Show, its origins were plain for all to see. Its designers saw no reason to hide its identity. The two-door 2 + 2 coupé bore a strong resemblance to the 327 and even sported a BMW-style kidney grille at the front, and circular insignia.

The Bristol engine was offered in four versions between 75 and 85bhp, but it soon grew much more powerful. Carburettors, cam profiles, crankshaft balancing, and some ingenious gas-flowing raised the power output for the road cars progressively to well over 100 horsepower. Later the capacity was increased for the proposed Bristol 220.

The 401, with smoother-shaped Touring-inspired bodywork, was introduced in 1949 and took Bristol into a new realm. It acquired a strong identity, carrying on in some respects where BMW had left off. With no pedigree of its own, it nurtured a reputation for careful engineering in a similar idiom to BMW's, and went to the best couturiers for its styling – the Superleggera body was a case in point.

Looking back on his friendship with the Aldingtons of AFN, Alex von Falkenhausen regretted not making more of BMW's British connections. 'The Bristol company made the BMW engine with better materials and it was very successful – especially in Formula B racing with Cooper. The best thing for AFN would have been for the Aldingtons to supply Bristol engines, and for me to make the car. It would have been unbeatable. Unfortunately it was difficult to keep in touch with people outside Germany then, and I

didn't think of it soon enough.' Resuming his links with AFN, von Falkenhausen designed a de Dion rear axle for the Le Mans Replica model. By 1954 Fritz Fiedler had returned from England, and soon made him an offer to return to BMW and run the racing department. 'It was only motorcycles at first, but I was quite glad to have a secure income. I was on the limit.' His erstwhile competitor, Ernst Loof of Veritas, also returned to BMW.

Motor sport revived in the late 1940s, not only on the track, but also on the road. This was the heyday of the long-distance rally in Europe, when roads were still relatively uncrowded, the motorway network still relatively undeveloped outside Germany and Italy, and even air travel not yet into its stride.

Setting off to the winter sunshine of Monte Carlo from the far corners of the Continent on snow and ice-bound roads was still a romantic adventure. The Bristol was just the car to do it in; sleek, fast, and strong. It was relatively light, however, at 1¼ tons, when something over 1½ was not unusual for Bentleys or Ford V8s. The Bristol 400 would do 0–60mph in a perfectly respectable 14.7 seconds, had a top speed of 94mph, and a fuel consumption of 21.4mpg according to a contemporary road-test.

The 400 distinguished itself by winning the 1948 Polish Rally, and taking third place in the 1949 Monte Carlo Rally. In 1952, Bristol established a racing department which not only modified engines but also made some high-quality racing cars, based on the abortive ERA G-Type chassis. A rather ugly coupé body was developed in the

Motif. The stylish bonnet louvres of Count Albrecht Goertz's 507 of 1956. Under-bonnet heat could no longer emerge from plain holes; they had to be chromed and latticed and embellished with the maker's name.

aircraft wind tunnel at Filton, featuring twin fins running down either side of the rear window. It did 142mph on the long runway at Filton, built for the Brabazon airliner, but failed in the 1953 Le Mans when the balance weights fell off the crankshaft.

Shortly afterwards, however, it gained a face-saving victory in the 2 litre class of the Rheims 12 Hours race, driven by Tommy Wisdom and Jack Fairman at an average speed of 92.65mph.

A much cleaner design was entered for the 1954 Le Mans and finished seventh, eight and ninth, winning the class and team prize. In some ways, it was a replay of the 1939 race; it was a perfectly-disciplined display of driving and running a team. All three cars finished within 68km (42 miles) of one another, yet the fastest of them covered only 307km (192 miles) more than the Touring BMW did in 1939, fifteen years earlier.

The 1955 Le Mans contenders were open sports cars with a fin at the rear. Once again the Bristol engine had been developed to produce a regular 150bhp. On the long Mulsanne straight the cars were timed at over 150mph, and the team performed with the same well-disciplined regularity once again. This time they failed to win their class at Rheims, but only narrowly, 9km (5½ miles) behind the winning Ferrari. More significantly, however, both were beaten handsomely by a 1½ litre 4-cam Porsche.

It was a sign that the old engine was at last reaching the end of the road, and even though one had produced 170bhp on test, Bristol could see that its time was up. In the wake of the 1955 Le

Mans disaster and the loss, in separate accidents, of two team drivers, the racing programme was abandoned.

The 402 Convertible and 403 followed, right through to the 406 of 1959, and as the decade progressed the Filton-produced cars became more luxurious and less sporty. By the time the 404 arrived in 1953, Bristol discarded the BMW kidney grille, no doubt mindful that the owner was now alive and kicking once more. In 1961 Bristol began to use large American Chrysler engines and the marque went its own way, to carve a niche in the luxury car market, without the BMW association.

Bristol always planned to make Grand Touring cars, leaving Frazer Nash to build sports cars in the style of the pre-war sports BMWs. Never people to shrink from publicity opportunities, the Aldingtons fitted a Frazer Nash grille to the Mille Miglia car, now with right-hand steering, and revealed this to a press eager to lavish praise on what they, at least, regarded as a British manufacturer.

There was no real attempt to hide its antecedents, nor was there ever any disagreement about the role of AFN and its sports car responsibilities within the partnership. But gradually the two parties went their separate ways, and in 1947 the association was formally dissolved. The separation was not acrimonious – Bristol continued to supply engines to AFN, and went on to provide special high-power FNS versions producing 100bhp.

The first true post-war Frazer Nash cars appeared at the 1948 London Motor Show, one of them the cycle-winged, torpedo-shaped 'High Speed' model, looking more Thirties than Fifties. Slung from a spring balance which showed that the chassis weighed a mere half a ton, with a 120bhp competition engine, it had a formidable performance.

The following year, H. J. Aldington and Norman Culpan took third place and won their class at Le Mans, a notable performance, from which the Le Mans Replica took its name. Over thirty were produced, and Frazer Nashes put up some stirring performances in the Mille Miglia, the Targa Florio, and at Sebring. They won Coupe des Alpes in 1951 and 1953, came third in the Tourist Trophy in 1950, 1951 and 1952, sixth in the 1950 Mille Miglia, fourth in the 1950 Giro di Sicilia, and won the 1951 Targa Florio.

The Bristol engine was used in the single-seater Cooper-Bristol with which Mike Hawthorn established himself as a pre-eminent driver, and brought him to the notice of Ferrari, leading to his world championship in 1958. The engine was also the motive source for countless other sports cars besides the Bristol 450. These included AC, Cooper, Lotus, Kieft, Lister, Tojeiro and Arnott as well as Frazer Nash.

It achieved remarkable results, but as the 1950s wore on the venerable six-cylinder was outclassed by modern designs. The last and most powerful Bristol was the BSX, which gave more than double the power of the original or its BMW forebear.

Throughout its distinguished career, the cross-pushrod arrangement contrived by Schleicher and Fiedler remained more or less intact. The engine suffered from being too tall, its downdraught carburettors on top making bonnet-top

air intakes a characteristic of its installation in cars such as the single-seat Cooper-Bristol and the Frazer Nashes. It was never known as a BMW, and by the time Bristol had lavished the best part of a decade's development on it, only the basic outline remained.

The last car that carried the Bristol name and the BMW heritage was the AC Ace of 1956–61. AC, of Thames Ditton, was the epitome of the conservative English sports car manufacturer, and had used John Weller's alloy OHC six-cylinder engine since 1919. Then, in 1953 it took over the design of a freelance engineer, John Tojeiro, of a successful sports racer with a Bristol engine, and produced a car that would become a classic.

Every inch a sports car, with exemplary roadholding, a formidable performance and commendable refinement, it was a car of which BMW could have been proud. The Ace and its derivative Aceca Coupé were beautifully proportioned and well finished. In its final form, with larger bore and longer stroke, the BS engine size had gone to 2216cc and 130bhp on the road – now almost thirty years after the design had been conceived.

The last AC left the production line in 1963, by which time BMW itself had moved far beyond the pre-war engine line and had started, for the first time since 1939, to enjoy real success. Bristol, and the other users and developers of the pre-war BMW had kept things going, handing on the torch throughout the dog days of the Forties and Fifties. And when BMW was ready to take it up again, the torch was still alight.

Bayerische Motoren Werke A.G.
München 46. Telegramme Bayernmotor

BMW poster art made the most of the badge.

The order by the American Military Government to raze the Milbertshofen plant was fortunately countermanded, and production allowed to continue under strict supervision. Kurt Donath was the Managing Director, and together with the Chairman of the Supervisory Board, Munich banker Dr Hans-Karl von Margoldt-Reiboldt, who had been appointed BMW's legal custodian in the aftermath of war, he was able to secure the company's survival. But it was a struggle through hostile and impecunious years.

With less than a thousand workers, the company lived from hand to mouth, scraping a fragile existence producing a few bicycles, pots and pans, baking utensils and agricultural machinery. The little band of survivors needed all its creative energy to scour the plant for raw materials that had not been taken in reparations. Older workers, more accustomed to the tidal fortunes of BMW following two wars, may have allowed themselves a wry smile when Donath accepted an order to produce railway brake sets.

Like everything else, BMW's finances were in a mess. As a trustee of the Deutsche Bank, Margoldt-Reiboldt deserves much of the recognition for enabling BMW to continue. Under normal circumstances, it would have been reckless to lend money to an organization so savagely pillaged, yet he negotiated a line of credit that allowed the development of the first real post-war product bearing the blue and white roundel.

Under occupation rules, BMW was forbidden to build a motorcycle of more than 250cc, however, when the R24, a

## A SECOND

## CHANCE

THE

MIRACLE

OF LIFE

1945–59

Another of Count Goertz's designs, this BMW 503 Convertible started turning heads in 1956. Later versions shunned the gearchange to the right of the steering column when the gearbox was repositioned behind the engine.

single-cylinder motorcycle was developed by Alfred Böning in 1947, the resulting orders gave BMW the encouragement it needed. Private transportation was hard to come by, and at 1,750 Marks, even such a basic machine found plenty of buyers.

Deliveries began in 1948, and turnover went up surprisingly fast. Over 7,000 motorcycles were made by 1950, the company employed over 8,700 people and it even managed to make a small profit. When Germany reformed its currency on 20 June 1948, BMW's capital lost value, but enthusiasm still brought results. In 1951, 1952 and 1954, new production records were achieved for BMW bikes, and larger twin-cylinder machines once again joined the programme.

By the end of 1949, war reparations were deemed paid up, and BMW once more planned to build cars. The engineers knew what they wanted to make, but BMW had no drawings and few tools, and raw material prices remained high. Unlike its competitors, Mercedes-Benz, Opel and Ford, BMW did not have the option of introducing warmed-up pre-war models; the car-producing plant was locked away seemingly for ever in Eisenach.

Forced to start afresh, engineers and directors debated what kind of car BMW should build. Logic in the austere economic climate suggested cheap, basic transportation like the Volkswagen. A small prototype, named variously the 331, under pre-war numbering, or 513 (post-war), was designed and built with a twin-cylinder motorcycle engine.

It was a pretty little coupé reminiscent of the Fiat Topolino, and was designed by Peter Schimanowski, a pre-war BMW stylist. It was well liked by the management, but the project was stillborn since it did not have four seats, and BMW's lack of capital for investment in tooling would have resulted in a high-cost, hand-built product for the most price-sensitive part of the market.

Another reason for the decision was Sales Director Hanns Grewenig's insistence that BMW should produce a recognizable 'calling card' – a luxury car consistent with the company's pre-war strategy. The new BMW would be a large luxury saloon, to be sold at a premium price, and another design was embarked on.

It is hard to imagine a less appropriate product for Germany, when basic commodities such as clothes and food were expensive and in short supply, and the priority for most people was simply meeting day-to-day needs. The only possible rationale for producing expensive cars was that in due course, when prosperity returned, the customers might be expected to multiply.

The result was duly displayed at the 1951 Frankfurt Show. The BMW 501 was a voluptuous, rather dull-looking car, but beneath its stately body it was at least entirely new, except for the engine. Its robust chassis consisted of deep box-section side-members extending almost the full width of the car, linked by four tubular crossbars, with a separate welded steel floorpan.

The double wishbone front suspension and live rear axle were both controlled by longitudinal torsion bars. Steering

Allied bombing devastated BMW's factories. By 1944 many buildings were unusable. Production continued in 'shadow' factories elsewhere, but before work could be resumed here in 1945, structures had to be repaired or demolished and rebuilt.

was by bevel gears jointed to a semi-circular rack and pinion. The four-speed gearbox was separate from the engine, connected by a short drive shaft, and placed almost under the front seats, to help distribute the not inconsiderable weight of the car evenly, and provide more foot room.

The mechanical weak link of Böning's design was the engine. BMW still had access to the moulds for the 326 pushrod six-cylinder, 2 litre engine, which had developed 50 horsepower in 1936–41. And since corners needed to be cut for reasons of both cost and time, it was pressed into service. A 65bhp version was designed and put into production.

Although the 501 was no longer than the 326 or its close relative the 327, and 11cm shorter than the 335, it weighed a good deal more. It soon became apparent that its 65 horses were not enough. A top speed of 84mph and

0–62mph sprint, if it can be called that, in 27 seconds, confirmed that more power was going to be needed.

The 501 met its objectives in space and comfort, and to complete the picture of luxury, a Becker radio was fitted as standard. The other luxury feature of the 501 was the price – DM15,000, for a performance that was decidedly leisurely, but at least it had a certain dignity.

Little of this was known when the lone prototype was revealed at Frankfurt. Although Schimanowski's body design was conservative, the new BMW created a great deal of interest. Alternatives designed by the coachbuilders Autenrieth, Michelotti and Pininfarina had been considered, but the home-grown, curvy, four-door saloon was preferred in the end.

It took eighteen months to get the 501 into production, and fewer than fifty reached their owners in 1952. The four-door bodies, every one black, were built painfully slowly by Baur Karosserie at Stuttgart, mostly by hand. But in 1953, with investment made available through Marshall Aid, BMW bought body presses and machine tools so that production could be substantially increased.

Unfortunately the large numbers of customers expected for the 501 failed to materialize, and BMW had to do something to fill its order books. A revised range was presented in March 1954, with a more powerful 72bhp engine. The 501A was essentially the same as its predecessor, but the price was reduced by nearly DM1,000.

It was followed by 501B, a lower specification model priced at DM12,680. In August prices were amended once again, car production doubled for the year and profits began at last, reaching their best for any year since the war at DM1.1 million.

Böning recognized, at an early stage of development, that the six-cylinder engine would not be strong enough to keep the customers happy for long. He started work on a V8, with Fritz Fiedler's help on his return from Bristol in 1951.

Its gestation period was prolonged owing to financial pressures and technical problems, but the all-aluminium, wet linered engine, Germany's first post-war V8, made its debut at the Geneva Show in March 1954. A 90-degree Vee, it bore similarities to its American counterparts but was much smaller, with a capacity of only 2580cc.

A pushrod engine with a narrow valve

angle, it was not designed to be a high-revving racing unit, but its output of 100bhp and substantial torque provided acceleration despite its great weight. When *The Autocar* came to try a 2.6 litre in 1956, the test staff found the engine so smooth they had to keep looking at the rev counter to reassure themselves that it was running.

Even allowing for some journalistic licence, this was praise indeed, and the car performed much as BMW had said it would, reaching 46mph and 71mph in second and third gears. Top speed was 101mph (162.5kph), and the 0–60mph time was 16.8 seconds, bearing out *The Autocar*'s view that it was '. . . a restful car to drive'. Of the steering column gearchange, it said, '. . . the type of mechanism employed tends to defeat any attempt at snap gearchanges.' The only real note of dissent was struck by the rear-hinged back doors, which were criticized on safety grounds. In every other respect the model was now ready to realize its potential.

At DM17,800, or £2,459 in Britain including tax, when a quality car such as the Riley Pathfinder was only £1,411 and a Jaguar XK140 Coupé £1,693, it was the premium end of the market, although a cheaper, lower specification 501 V8 was soon offered to broaden its appeal. Further changes were brought in for 1955, with BMW beginning to display, at last, some of its pre-war light-footedness, by offering an almost bewildering range of variants.

First of all, the old six-cylinder was given a final shot in the arm by increasing the bore by two millimetres. The 501, now with a displacement of 2077cc retained its 72bhp, but its increased torque made it lively enough to remain saleable until 1958. After that, only V8-engined cars were offered. These were given a revised body, with a fashionable wrap-around rear window, and even more chrome embellishment.

Later in the year an enlarged V8 of 3168cc, giving a healthy 120bhp, was offered in the 502, and higher compression ratios and twin choke carburetters raised this still further to 140bhp in the 1957 3.2 litre Super, making it possible to cruise the *autobahn* at an imposing 110mph.

There were few more outward changes to the 'Baroque Angels', as they were affectionately nicknamed after the voluptuous, rather fleshy ladies carved into the cornices of so many Bavarian churches. In 1960, for the first time on a German car, vacuum-assisted disc front brakes became standard equipment. These were necessary, particularly for the ultimate 'angel', the 3200S of 1961. With a 160bhp development of the V8 engine, the car was now capable of almost 120mph, at a price very little higher than that of the first 502 in 1955.

Well over 23,000 Baroque Angels were produced between 1952 and 1963, of which 14,165 were V8s. They included a few very special two- and four-door coupé and cabriolet models by Baur and Autenrieth, an exclusive product built to special order. The range may not be highly regarded by enthusiasts, but it is notable for its durability, among other things. It was the first post-war BMW design; it survived through a major crisis in the company's history, and it was still being produced even when BMW was back on the high road to success.

Back in 1955, however, BMW still had big plans for the future, despite the warning signs of impending financial disaster.

Now that the V8 engine was available, BMW's directors pursued every up-market niche they could think of. More than that, Sales Director Hanns Grewenig eyed the profitable American market. After all, he reasoned, what more could the Los Angeles boulevardier want than European style, together with the robust power of a V8?

Grewenig pressed hard for a 502-based sports car, but his more realistic co-directors were reluctant to commit themselves to further investment. The turning-point came in 1952, when Mercedes-Benz revealed the 300SL sports car, and the doubters were at once won over to Grewenig's point of view.

The rear suspension of the BMW 700 set the pattern for many BMWs to come. The twin trailing arms located the rear wheels firmly and held them upright in bump and rebound.

BMW was encouraged by the enthusiastic Max Hoffman, an Austrian who had emigrated to the USA early in the war, and in the 1950s held the import concessions for both Mercedes-Benz and BMW. Hoffman played an important role in the conception of BMW's sports car, the success of which rested very much on the large, wealthy American market.

Hoffman greatly admired the work of Count Albrecht Goertz, an industrial designer who worked for Studebaker before setting up his own styling studio in New York. By November 1954, Goertz had prepared two studies, both of which were accepted by BMW, and Grewenig found himself with not one, but two new sports cars.

There was another contender, a proposal by Ernst Loof, formerly of Veritas, now works development engineer at BMW, for a 507 two-seater on a 502 chassis with a 2.6 litre V8. He had a prototype built by Baur in Stuttgart, where cabriolet 501s were made. Loof's creation was long, low and rather bulbous at the front, with something of the Nash-Healey about it. By the standards of the early 1950s it probably looked quite good, if undistinguished.

Loof promoted it vigorously, and entered it in a concours d'élégance at Bad Neuenlich in September 1954, hinting that this was a review of a new BMW sports car. It was the only time it was ever seen in public. Goertz's design had better proportions, and an elegance that Loof's never had.

At the Frankfurt Show in late 1955, BMW proudly displayed the 503 and 507 prototypes alongside the 501 and

The ultimate Baroque Angel, the imposing, and ultimately unsuccessful State Limousine. Only a handful were ever made, and only used on provincial, rather than federal service.

502. Although they came from the same design studio at the same time, the two newcomers were remarkably different. The 503 shared the 502 chassis and 111.6-inch wheelbase. It also had the middle gearbox with a steering column gearchange and the same suspension.

Powered by the 7.5:1 compression ratio 140bhp engine, the 503 was no lightweight, despite its alloy body. In fact it weighed just about as much as the heaviest 3200 saloon, and it was only through better aerodynamics and different gearing that it accelerated faster and managed to keep the 118mph top speed.

It was also a very long coupé with 2 + 2 seating squeezed between a seemingly endless bonnet and a cavernous boot. It possessed some characteristics of Pininfarina cars of the time, and might have become a classic in its own right, had the 507 not appeared at the same time.

The 507 was a real beauty, well proportioned, with a grace not always seen in sports cars. It was the first really memorable car BMW had produced since the war, and marked the firm's return to the exclusive ranks of car manufacturers whose products are accorded classic status – not by decree or by the deliberations of a committee, but by enthusiasts to whom quality is important.

Then, as ever, keen drivers were looking for quality of operation, doors that shut reassuringly firmly, an engine that ran smoothly, glossy paintwork, well-made interiors – and they were coming round to the view that they would find it in BMWs.

For the 507, Goertz shortened the 502 chassis by 14 inches, and reduced the cross-members to three. As a result the gearbox, now a close ratio design, was attached to the engine, and the steering column gearchange, a curious aberration afflicting not only BMW but a number of European manufacturers who had been told by their American importers that it was necessary, was at last abandoned. The repositioned gearbox had instead a more precise-feeling, sporting floor gearchange.

Like the 503, the 507 had large 16-inch wheels and 502 front suspension, while the rear axle was firmly located by a Panhard rod, and an anti-roll bar. The 503 chassis was a robust perimeter frame which compensated for the strength lost through not having a roof. Mercedes-Benz had dealt with the problem of beam strength by building a multi-tube chassis with deep sills, which needed the famous gull-wing doors because ordinary doors would have been too shallow for people to climb through easily.

BMW's solution was a strong fabricated tubular framework extended to the outer edges of the car, providing an immensely strong structure which held up on its own, and allowed full-length cutaway doors.

The 507 was light, where its stable-mates were heavy. The engine had a high lift camshaft, a high compression ratio and polished internals, a means of achieving a high rate of gas flow into the cylinders, which gave it an impressive power output of 150bhp at 5,000rpm. Depending on the rear axle ratio selected by the customer, it could reach 118, 124 or 137mph. The choice was between brisk acceleration and a slower maximum, or less pull, and a turn of speed that made it one of the fastest production cars in the world.

The beautiful Goertz bodywork had been designed as both a convertible and a hardtop. The wide, squat, kidney-shaped grille suited a low front, and the wings swept in a lazy line to the back of the doors, where the upper body rose again, gently, to clear the rear wheels. Speed creases, leading from the top of both front and rear wheel arches, emphasized the economical grace of the whole car.

Both cars, particularly the 507, should have been runaway successes. Hoffman expected to sell 5,000 a year at $5,000 each. Unfortunately BMW could not get down to the price. There were not enough machine tools, so both cars were virtually hand-made. By the time they reached the showrooms, in May and November 1956 respectively, the 503 sold for DM29,500 and the 507 for DM26,500. In America the 507 price was almost $9,000.

Predictably, they did not sell in large numbers. Only 412 examples of the 503 were made, and 253 of the 507. Both added great lustre to the BMW image, but not enough were sold to cover their costs.

BMW's final fling, before the financial alarm bells began to sound once again, was the 'Grosser' BMW 505. Two prototypes were built to challenge Mercedes-Benz in the 'Chancellor' class. Featuring a wheelbase nine inches longer than the 502 and powered by the new 120bhp V8 engine, the 505 was aimed directly at the prestigious state car market which Mercedes dominated.

Its high, square-cut styling was by Michelotti, and the bodywork was executed by the Swiss Ghia-Aigle concern. Unfortunately, after Chancellor Konrad Adenauer sat in the back, and knocked his hat off getting out, the 505 headed straight for the museum. Dignitaries, it was felt, needed bigger doors, so the sole production 505 was downgraded to local government level, and used only for state visitors to Bavaria. Yet the very existence of the 'Chancellor' car put BMW on a new footing in the German motor industry. The implicit challenge to Mercedes would never be forgotten by either side.

The tide now began to run against BMW. Germany's middle class was getting rich and, quite suddenly, demand for motorcycles declined. They were no longer needed for mere transport, and after so many years of record production, output fell from almost 30,000 to 23,000 in 1955. The dramatic downturn continued in 1956 and 1957, when 15,500 and then a mere 5,429 machines left the factory.

It was many years before motorcycle production would recover, and by the time it did, in 1977, the market had changed. Motorcycling had become something more than transportation; it had become a leisure pursuit, and the motorcycle division would never again be BMW's primary source of income.

BMW seemed to see the trouble ahead, and as the motorcycle market declined, began moving towards high-volume car production. At the 1955 Frankfurt Motor Show, it displayed for the first time a novel vehicle which would do comfortably over 40 mpg. Carrying the

BMW's answer to the fuel crises of the 1950s, the Isetta. With a simple tubular chassis and a single cylinder air cooled engine, it did over 50mph (85kph) and 70mpg (4 litres/100kms).

**600** *ein e*

*ter BMW*

BMW badge was a strange egg-shaped miniature, called the Isetta.

BMW had repeated history and once again taken out a licence, as a means of getting into production quickly, this time with a tiny two-seater known affectionately as *'das rollende Ei'* – the rolling egg. It had been conceived by the Italian Iso concern in 1952, and BMW approached the owner, Count Rivolta (later to make high-performance sports cars), who sold not only the production rights of the Iso, but much of the body tooling as well.

BMW changed Count Rivolta's design by fitting the air-cooled, 247cc four-stroke engine from the R25 motorcycle, so the Isetta offered bubble car enthusiasts 12bhp in place of the 9bhp produced by its Italian two-stroke. Driving through a four-speed motorcycle gearbox to twin rear wheels placed 20½ inches apart, the extra power gave the Isetta a top speed of 53mph and achieved the 0–50mph dash in what must have seemed like a fortnight. However, the light, frugal carriage was not intended for high performance. The best thing it had to offer was 43mpg, together with its price – a mere DM2,580, which was only 500 more than the R25 motorcycle.

In the mid-1950s there was good reason to be frugal. The President of Egypt's seizure of the Suez Canal, in July 1956, was the culmination of a series of political events that led to oil shortages in Europe, and a micro car craze that reached its peak with some peculiar vehicles of which the Isetta was typical.

The best that can be said about the Isetta's front-opening door carrying the

Once the Isetta was stretched and a proper fourth wheel added, it carried four people – but only just. They would seldom be quite so much at ease as those in this 1958 publicity shot.

steering wheel and column, was that it enabled the driver to run front-on to the pavement and step straight out. It also gave the manufacturer useful photo opportunities with celebrities such as Cary Grant and Stirling Moss. To meet the demand for more power, BMW installed a 296cc engine, which gave all of one horsepower more.

BMW made several body changes in 1956, and in 1958 developed a three-wheel version later assembled in Britain by a new company, BMW Concessionaires of Brighton. The modification enabled the vehicle to qualify as a motorcycle in order to be taxed more cheaply.

Between 1955 and 1962, no fewer than 161,728 Isetta 250 and 300 models were sold, making it by far BMW's best-selling product to date. Despite such huge sales however, the profit contribution from each Isetta was tiny. The other problem was that fashion markets are fickle, and the new middle classes needed more room. When in due course the fuel crisis passed, and petrol became plentiful and cheap once again, they began to look for something better.

BMW's interim answer was the 600 model, which looked like a stretched Isetta, but was more car than bubble. It was 21½ inches longer and had the wheels at the corners, or near the corners at any rate, the rear ones being still two inches closer together than those at the front. It retained a front-opening door, and also had one on the right side for entry to the rear seat. With a twin-cylinder 582cc motorcycle engine, the 600 was able to cruise at 60mph and give 40mpg. Nearly 35,000

were produced in a short run between December 1957 and 1959.

The 600's legacy, for every BMW until the M1 of 1978, was an independent rear suspension system of trailing arms. Unlike the swinging half-axles of the 3/20 in 1932, these A-shaped arms with coil springs and telescopic dampers achieved independent springing of each rear wheel, taking the drive through jointed half-shafts, and kept the tread of the tyre flat on the road. Gone was the squirming and edgy handling of an earlier era, and the system was such a success that it was adopted in principle for almost every production BMW from then on. Although they wanted to develop a real mid-size car, the BMW directors could not raise sufficient bank support for the development of a 1300cc engine and an entirely new body. Small loans were obtained, and a Bremen timber merchant, Hermann Krages, purchased a large shareholding which enabled BMW to develop the 600 theme. The resulting 700 used an enlarged 30bhp version of the BMW flat-twin, which was put into a neat coupé styled by Giovanni Michelotti.

BMW liked it, but wanted something with more room in the back, so, with Michelotti's help, a saloon was also evolved. Two feet longer than the 600, it proved to be a genuine four-seater. With a door on either side, a bonnet (at the back to give access to its rear-mounted engine), and a boot, it was the first BMW to combine chassis and body in a single unitary construction.

The light weight of the 700 allowed the saloon to reach 74mph, and the more rakish coupé 78mph. This level of performance, combined, with 33mpg,

The immoderate amount of chrome in the 1950s gave way to the textures of light alloy for the wheels of a later generation.

BMW's return to real cars. Michelotti designed both the 700 saloon and coupé of 1959–65 on the same hull, but the coupé had a shorter roof. Bonnet stripes and the hooped bumper (top) mark the longer 700LS.

presented an interesting challenge to the ageing Volkswagen Beetle. It was only prices of DM4,760 for the saloon and DM5,300 for the coupé that put larger numbers of buyers off.

By 1954, Alex von Falkenhausen had rejoined BMW as Competitions Manager, which meant a return to motorcycle racing and record-breaking. Von Falkenhausen used the 502, 507, 600 and even the Isetta in sport. The 507 was developed to produce 170bhp, and had sports suspension, disc brakes and under-car aerodynamics developed for it. Stuck and von Falkenhausen used one in minor events, but it was in a class against Maseratis, Ferraris and Porsches which were built for racing. The engine, moreover, was not very suitable for tuning – 'it had very small parallel valves and really the car was too heavy,' said von Falkenhausen.

Of the 502 he said, 'It was a handful, too heavy, but a good car', and of the 700, 'It was very competitive and won many races but the Mini Coopers became almost unbeatable in the end.' Hans Stuck won the GT class of a number of European hill-climbs with the 507, then by 1957 von Falkenhausen had been appointed the chief of engine design and put in charge of development of the 700. Given his enthusiasm for racing, it was hardly surprising that a sporting version was developed in 1960, producing 40bhp and doing 83mph. Handling was improved by tighter suspension and a rear anti-roll bar, making the 700 a practical and inexpensive racing model which enjoyed numerous victories in races, hill-climbs and rallies.

The 700 proved yet another ingredient

of BMW's return to esteem, and although there was a long way to go – the cars were still small, and they were only generating small profits – morale was high and the pace was speeding up.

Between 1959 and 1965, nearly 190,000 BMW 700s left the Munich production lines, including a Luxus model a foot longer, and 2,600 Baur Cabriolets. Thus the 700 became in its turn the best-selling BMW in the company's fifty-year history. There was, however, another miracle to come before the survival not only of the 700 but of BMW as a whole was secure.

Between 1946 and 1955 there had been five years of profit and five of loss – the results were never far from break-even. In 1956, despite the high production rate of the Isetta, the company started to lose money at an alarming rate. The extent of BMW's dependence on motorcycles became all too apparent as sales dropped, and although turnover continued on an apparently healthy upward trend from DM36.5 million in 1950 to DM138 million in 1955 and 195.3 million in 1958, the financial position was not good.

In 1955, BMW revived the Allach facility, under the name BMW Triebwerkbau, to build General Electric jet turbines (used for the unfortunate Lockheed Starfighter in the new *Luftwaffe*) under licence. Then, in an attempt to recoup the losses from the other parts of the business, it sold half its holdings in it to MAN, the truck manufacturer, for DM25 million, but very soon withdrew from aero-engine operation altogether. The new subsidiary had only been making things worse, and the losses mounted, seemingly inexorably, by DM6.5 million in 1956 and 1957, then by DM12 million in 1958. Kurt Donath, who presided over BMW's most difficult rebirth, retired in 1957, handing over to the Finance Director, Dr Heinrich Richter-Brohm.

Confidence in Richter-Brohm did not run high. The BMW management team knew what it had to do to survive – build a real mid-size car – but it could not raise the money. Krages withdrew from the BMW board in February 1959, dissatisfied with progress. Then the Bavarian state government offered a DM10 million loan on the understanding that Richter-Brohm resigned.

Predictably this was refused, as were advances from a number of predatory suitors from the USA, Britain and Germany. The directors were convinced that the next edition of the 700 would save the company, but the banks were not prepared to take the risk. They proposed instead to re-structure the company, and halve the value of existing shares. This was to be followed by a new share issue, which would be open only to the banks and Daimler-Benz AG.

What the banks were trying to contrive was a thinly-veiled merger with Mercedes, and it might well have gone through despite the protests from small shareholders, many of whom were loyal BMW dealers, but for the vigorous defence they were prepared to mount. Their first move was to secure an adjournment of the critical meeting called to discuss the proposal.

By the time it reconvened later the same day, their lawyer had discovered an item in the accounts, indicating that the development costs for the 700 had been written down in only one year, instead of over the longer amortization period that was customary. Richter-Brohm resigned, taking much of the Deutsche Bank influence with him, and a further adjournment allowed time for a new shareholder to join the rebellious ranks.

Buying the Krages share, Dr Herbert Quandt and his brother Harold installed Gerhard Wilcke on the BMW board, and took a direct interest in the company's development. The Quandt family gradually gained a controlling stake in BMW and remained major shareholders.

The 1950s had been a time of great uncertainty. In the years leading up to 1959 was it despair or determination to survive that existed within BMW? Alex von Falkenhausen described the mood to Chris Willows: 'I think the main problem was that every year we seemed to have a new board of directors. They changed very quickly. It was very difficult to come into contact with a new director – they were all in despair. But the people under the directors wanted to do something so they tried very hard.'

The Quandts brought more than money to BMW. They offered a new sense of direction, something the firm had not enjoyed since the years of Franz-Josef Popp. Under the new regime which they gradually put in place, BMW emerges from a low point in its history, on the way to one of the most successful revivals in post-war European manufacturing industry.

The Frankfurt International Automobile Ausstellung of 1961 was BMW's turning-point. It was always an important motor show, a barometer of the health and strength of the German motor industry in the sprawling halls of the Frankfurt Exhibition Centre. This was the scene for the introduction of a new car that would pave the way to the recovery and the long-term profitability of BMW. It would take time, but once the new 1500 model went on sale, with its good proportions, its lively turn of speed and its exemplary handling, the road ahead lay open.

Making a car ready for Frankfurt was one thing. Making the production facilities ready was quite another, and it was fully a year before customers would see one. The delay in getting a car into production was not a new experience for BMW. In 1951, the 501 took just as long to get under way.

Delays were not the 1500's only problem. It had been developed in some haste, and on a tight budget, and many of the customers who did eventually take delivery soon began rather to wish they hadn't. Gearbox and back axle failures were the worst of the car's quality problems, and BMW engineers had to get to work putting things right.

Quite apart from the German market, Hoffman had now set up dealerships in the United States, where the clientele was demanding a high-quality product. The Detroit leviathans were going through a bad patch of indifferent roadholding, wallowy suspension and poor braking. Yet they were well made and for the most part reliable, so although the good handling of small

## THE

## SECOND

## COMING

Before rear-hinged doors were outlawed as dangerous, the big 502 saloon's door handles came together at the centre pillar. Chauffeurs could alight quickly and open the back door for the passenger.

Fred M Zeder's Chrysler Airflow of 1934 finds an echo in the BMW 501 of 1952. Pininfarina admired it, but rich customers were thin on the ground in post-war Germany.

European cars meant that they were catching on as an alternative, they had to match the Americans for quality.

BMW had some false starts on the way to the 1500. Further development of the 700 had been thought about, and a 1 litre version built, but there were limits to the weight which could be put at the rear of the little car without affecting its handling. The Isetta was still in production, but due to go, and the V8s were on their last legs. Something new was needed in the middle ground, between the Rolling Egg and the Baroque Angels, and just at the right moment a gap in the market opened up when Borgward failed.

Carl Borgward made Hansa cars before the war, and continued in the mini-car era after 1945, with Hansa-Lloyd and Goliath cars in Bremen. The first Borgward 1500 made a strong impression at the 1949 Geneva Motor Show, for not only was it the first truly new post-war German design, with a smart, full-width body, but it was also well built. By the time the unit-construction Isabella appeared in 1954, it had achieved an even more formidable reputation. The Touring Sport (TS) sold well, competed successfully in rallies, and appealed strongly to the emerging middle class as an extremely capable home-grown German car, to rival the US-owned Opel or Ford.

The last Borgward was a six-cylinder, 100bhp, 2.3 litre saloon with air suspension, but it was in production for less than a year before the firm collapsed in 1961. It shows what a loyal market Borgwards had built up, that even after regular production ceased, they were still being put together from remaining spares. The final indignity for a fine series of cars came when the rights were bought by a Mexican firm, which carried on making Isabellas for several years, with conventional suspension in place of the sophisticated air springs.

First of the New Class the 1500 of 1962–64 took a year to get into production, but it was soon established as the forerunner of an entire dynasty of BMWs.

BMW could be fitted neatly into the space vacated by the respected but ultimately ill-fated Borgward. It was wholly German, it had an equally good sporting pedigree, and although memories had to stretch back to the late 1930s to remember the best bits, the new generation had been sufficiently exposed to cars such as the Veritas and the AFM and the Bristol, which had enough BMW in them to be regarded as lineal descendents. BMW knew it was never going to compete with Ford or Opel in the volume market, nor with Mercedes-Benz in the luxury market – not yet anyway – but Borgward had demonstrated that there was a niche for well-made, premium-priced, fast saloon cars. It was the niche BMW had occupied in the 1930s, and there seemed no reason why it could not occupy it again.

The only obstacle was still BMW's chronic shortage of money, which was why there was something of a hiatus between announcing the new 1500, in which Herbert Quandt believed so passionately, and getting it into production.

Alex von Falkenhausen played a major role in the 1500's success: 'The Directors wanted a 1300. It took a lot of work and persuasion to make it a 1500. At the time a 2 litre car was a big car, unlikely to sell in big numbers – there was only Mercedes. Others like Borgward and Opel had 1500s, so BMW hardly dared make a 2 litre.' However, von Falkenhausen proved that a clever engineer can influence events surreptitiously. 'I thought we needed to have a good 2 litre. So when they agreed to build a 1500, I designed it so it could easily be made an 1800 and then, with a new casting technique, a 2 litre. It was only a year before they wanted a 1600, then in another year an 1800.'

These engines powered all the four-door 1500–2000 range, then the two-door 1600–2002 series, the 3 series, and the four-cylinder 5 series and were only halted when a new 1.6 litre M40 engine was introduced at the end of 1988. In all, 3.5 million M10/12 series engines were produced. On the race-track they powered touring cars, sports cars, and a succession of F2 champions culminating in Nelson Piquet's world championship-winning Brabham BT52.

Did von Falkenhausen foresee the potential the 1500 engine had for motor sport when he designed it? 'I thought the block was good for 200, even 300bhp, but I never thought it would take 1,000 horsepower,' he told Chris Willows.

The 1500 was wheeled on to the stand at Frankfurt with unabashed self-confidence. Nobody yet knew that the cast-iron block of its upright four-cylinder engine would find its way into a Grand Prix car and win the world championship, or that its aluminium cylinder head with a single chain-driven

overhead camshaft would become something of a classic. Meanwhile, it was simply a well-proportioned small saloon with MacPherson strut independent front suspension, and a development of the semi-trailing arms at the rear, first seen on the little 700.

In 1962, confident that the 1500 would be a success, BMW dropped the Isetta with a certain amount of relief, and in 1963 the last of the Baroque Angels went as well. The only survivors of the old range were the 3.2 litre 3200CS, a Bertone coupé giving a hint of coupés still to come and owing something to the old 507, and the remaining 700 models.

After the 'Angels' had finally taken flight, BMW was left with a range of cars with four-cylinder engines based on that 1½ litre of 1961. The 1800TI was presented in 1963 with an extra 20bhp, and canted at thirty degrees to reduce its height. Most of the increase in

Das ist Ihr Wagen: Geräumiger Innenraum mit vier bequemen Sitzen· viel Platz für Gepäck· lebendiger, laufruhiger Viertakt-motor· 30 PS· vollsynchronisiertes Viergang-getriebe . . . und eine elegante, begeisternde Form -natürlich ein BMW 700

BMW 700

Michelotti's 700 had crisp, clean lines. Luggage, spare wheel, and fuel tank were all under the front bonnet.

BMW 2000 CS

capacity was obtained by making the stroke 9mm longer, and the canted engine fitted tidily, even when it was redesigned for 1965, with two quite large Weber carburettors on the side.

The saloons became well established with two and four doors, selling successfully despite the 1800 acquiring a reputation for faulty gearboxes. By the mid-1960s there were no fewer than ten versions of the sturdy little four-cylinder.

It was reworked and changed, bored out to give a capacity of 1991cc, and installed in a modified body shell with better suspension and bigger brakes. The handling was more consistent, and the appearance subtly improved in a way that would become another BMW hallmark, with no fundamental changes in style. Continuity of this sort was regarded as important for the dignity of the BMW line, and reassuring for the

customer. It helped him believe that he was buying a certain integrity, and not just the latest, fashionable trend.

There was also a pretty coupé, the 2000CS, with 120 horsepower and manual transmission, or 100 horsepower and ZF automatic. It was the first coupé of the so-called New Class in 1965; and was designed not by an Italian styling house, but in Munich by Wilhelm Hofmeister, and the old 3200CS was discarded.

For 1966, BMW's fiftieth anniversary, the custom of mixing the ingredients of different models was applied to a new 2000, which had the New Class body and chassis, and the 2 litre engine from the coupé, together with rectangular headlights and smart new tail-lights. The 2000TI was a 120 horsepower version, without the styling changes on the grounds that some customers would like the extra power, but would

*Following pages:*
BMW elegance at the Frankfurt Motor Show of 1955. In a display designed to rival the Mercedes-Benz exhibit — the Mille Miglia winning 300SLR of Stirling Moss, BMW displayed Goertz's 503, with its graceful assortment of grilles.

Large smooth engine in a compact car, the 2002ti, one of the cars that changed the post-war fortunes of BMW. Introduced in 1968, it set the pattern for the range of cars that became the 3-Series.

be prepared to put up with the old round headlights, if they could have the car cheaper.

A few months later came the TI-lux, which had the newer 2000 body features, but cost DM1,000 more. No marketing ploy was neglected to sell cars, and the response was extremely satisfactory. Two-door down-market cars fitted with engines from the next-biggest model in the range at once became up-market. It was a recipe that worked before and would work again and again for BMW.

The most important birthday presen-tation, however, was the smaller two-door 1600–2, the first of the most successful BMW range yet. In its fiftieth year, BMW was not only firmly second in the German luxury car sales league behind Daimler-Benz, but the increase was steep and sustained. Following the

introduction of the new cars, German registrations of BMWs in 1966 soared by thirty per cent, and sales to all markets by twenty-seven per cent, over the 1965 figure, to over DM755 million. More than 74,000 cars were made, which was 6,000 more than in 1965, and in 1967 this increased again to 87,618, and reached 100,000 in 1968.

The recipe worked especially well in America, where the 1600-2 was introduced at $2,500, and *Car & Driver* called it 'The best small sedan we ever drove; just like driving a 1300 Alfa Romeo Veloce built by Germans.' Of Max Hoffman, it wrote, 'He has probably made more money from the imported car business than any other individual in our time. Now, with the BMW 1600 he has the best economy car ever offered to an undeserving American public, and he seems to be firmly and permanently established as its distributor. Mr Hoffman will no doubt get richer, and America will be a better place for it.'

As it happens, Mr Hoffman was not permanently established as the distributor for BMW, or for all his other profitable European lines either. By 1974, after the United States had become its most important export market, BMW replaced him with a wholly owned subsidiary, BMW of North America Inc., after a lengthy legal battle. There was a certain amount of disillusion in Bavaria when a survey by the new firm revealed that while Hoffman had certainly ensured that BMW was well known to the hard core of American car buffs, the public at large mostly thought the initials stood for British Motor Works.

By 1968, the 2002 had established BMW as a force to be reckoned with in the United States, a market that would

be vital to its continued development. It amply justified the confidence BMW had shown in its continued prosperity by taking over Glas at Dingolfing, in Lower Bavaria.

Hans Glas had made agricultural machinery but, like Borgward, when Germany was on the move again, had taken the opportunity to set it running on very small wheels. The Goggomobil was one of the micro-cars of the fuel-frugal Fifties, a tiny twin-cylinder, two-stroke-engined car that led to larger models, much as the 700 grew out of the Isetta.

By 1961, Glas cars were enterprisingly engineered four-cylinder, four-stroke saloons and coupés. They were first to drive the camshaft of a large-scale production engine by means of a toothed belt. Commonplace in later years, this was regarded with some

Inherited from Glas in Dingolfing, the short-lived 1600GT had a body designed by Frua. Fewer than 1,300 were made, with BMW engines and kidney-shaped grilles, before the model disappeared.

The 1967 BMW 1600 Convertible. The open four-seater echoed pre-war touring cars, and reappeared in the BMW range beside saloon counterparts.

scepticism in 1961, when chain or gear drives were universal.

In 1965 there was a pretty Glas V8 2600 with a striking coupé body designed by Frua, the Italian coachbuilder, in which overhead camshafts on both banks of cylinders were driven by toothed belts. Following the BMW take-over, this engine and the 1700s which briefly continued to be sold as BMWs were discontinued. The Goggomobil was dropped as well, after over a quarter of a million of them had been made, for what BMW really wanted at Dingolfing were the labour force and the production facilities for a new range.

The old order was still not played out, however, and America had an important role to play in a new model that would become a BMW classic. In 1968, laws controlling exhaust emission were established for imported cars, which could have presented problems for the 1600-/2ti, and at Hoffman's

instigation Munich, following its now well-established practice of putting the next-biggest engine into a smaller-bodied car, put a 2 litre into the two-door 1600.

It could not be called a 2000 without risk of confusion, so it was labelled 2002, and despite the loss of power compared with a non-emission-controlled 2 litre, even when it was de-smogged, it was a huge success. The light body and big engine gave the 2002 a good turn of speed even in its single carburettor form. 'One of modern civilization's best ways to get somewhere sitting down,' wrote David E. Davis in Car & Driver. When it acquired fuel injection it would do 115mph, and it became the staple model on the US market for eight years.

Yet the most had now been made of BMW's splendid little four-cylinder engine; its capabilities were clearly not infinite, and sooner or later something else would need to be done. If BMW was to expand the way it wanted, and fill the production capacity it had bought itself at Dingolfing, one obvious course was to do as in 1933, and introduce a new six.

Bernhard Osswald had become Director of Engineering in 1966, and taking the four-cylinder as his model, but with a new combustion chamber, he and von Falkenhausen drew up a 2494cc 150bhp, and 2788cc 170bhp six-cylinder engine of remarkable smoothness and notable economy. At the same time a new coupé was announced in which, with

commendable thrift, BMW had mounted the new engine in place of the 2000CS's four-cylinder, lengthening the front, changing the grille, but keeping the old pressings for the remainder.

The result was a surprisingly homogeneous whole, which looked right from the start, and formed the basis of many coupés to come. The body was built, and the car assembled from components shipped in from other BMW factories, by Karmann at Osnabrück. It marked a further stage in BMW evolution, and a gradual climb up-market in America, where the new 2800CS sold for nearly $9,000.

The kidney grille is reduced to a cipher. The proportions have changed with the dictates of fashion, as on the 1602 model of 1966-77.

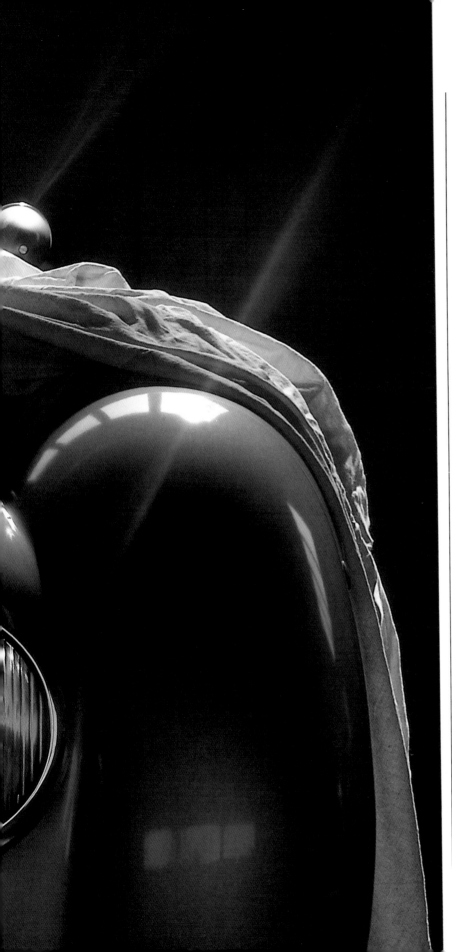

Fittingly enough, for a firm born into such a competitive business, BMW seemed to attract competitive people. There was always a cadre of executives convinced that competition was the best place not only to show off aircraft and motorcycles and cars, but to develop them as well. Competition, in both motor sport and record-breaking, was regarded as an incentive to the engineers to build an aero engine that could go higher, or a car or motorcycle that could go faster than anybody else's.

It was this spirit that inspired Zeno Diemer to new heights in 1919, and enabled the three Austin-BMW-Dixis of Buchner, Kandt, and Wagner ten years later to win the team prize and a Gold Cup in the Alpine Trial. In 1931, in a 10,000km rally from Berlin to Spain, and back again through Italy, Yugoslavia and Austria, three works BMW 3/15s and one private team survived a punishing event and won the 2 litre class.

BMW began to score more worthwhile successes with the first six-cylinder engines in the 315/1, when a team of three won their class in the 1934 German Rally. Then came Henne's famous victory in the 328 at the Nürburgring, which brought the make into racing, and in 1939 the stirring performance at Le Mans. The Mille Miglia cars of 1940 were landmarks in the history of the sports car, and, as with many of BMW's most successful competition vehicles, owed something to the aircraft designer's discipline of obtaining maximum power with the minimum weight and the most trustworthy durability.

It was not be an unblemished record of

# BOLD

# BMWs

## THE

## RACING

## STORY

The Mille Miglia BMW suffered the depredations of war, English racing, and years of neglect until Michael Bowler rescued it in 1967. Recreated rather than restored by BMW, it is probably rather better than new, but not much of it ever raced in the Mille Miglia.

Turning point for BMW. The poster for the Eifel races, where Ernst Henne and the 328 made their mark.

success, however, particularly when it came to Grand Prix racing. Yet the breadth of BMW's competitive spirit came in due course to support one of the world's most consistently successful, and longest established motor sporting departments.

For some of its greatest triumphs, BMW reverted to its role of an engine manufacturer, and left others to provide the car. It was as an engine supplier that BMW made the 1983 combination of Nelson Piquet and the Brabham BT52 the first turbocharged Formula 1 Grand Prix world champions.

In Formula 2, BMW won six European championships with the iron block, four-cylinder, 2 litre engine, developed for the 1962 production 1500 saloon. An even more significant link with the production cars was provided by the 1.5 litre block of the Grand Prix motor from the same model, which became a 1499cc turbocharged showcase for 1980s technology such as Bosch Motronic management. The castings were carefully aged and lightened by some 5–7kg, before becoming a racing item, and it was the only engine in Grand Prix racing for many years which had, as its basis, the actual material of a production car.

Some production BMWs owed their origin to the racing department. The M3 came about through the European and world touring car championships, a branch of motor sport which fell into neglect, and later disappeared altogether. European saloon car racing was tough, with races up to twenty-four hours long, but BMW was consistently successful in it from the start of the series in 1963, and between 1966 and 1988, 27 championships fell to BMW,

eleven to cars and sixteen to BMW drivers.

Cars such as the 635 won Dieter Quester the title in 1983, his fourth European Championship in a BMW. Roberto Ravaglia, in the 635CSi Coupé, then the M3 and the so-called M3 Evolution, won the only world touring car championship ever held, in 1987, together with three European drivers' titles.

The link between BMW's success before the war and its prowess afterwards was the BMW 328, and the AFM and Veritas cars which it inspired. They not only kept the BMW engine actively racing, but kept key people in racing, so that by the time the courteous but determined von Falkenhausen rejoined BMW in 1954, he had a useful track record in post-war racing behind him.

He knew enough to ensure that BMW had the best driving talent, to make the most of the limited horsepower of the available cars. Sometimes it was as little as 56 or 85bhp, but he put drivers such as Hans Stuck Senior and promising newcomers such as Jacky Ickx and Hubert Hahne into BMWs.

It was a process that took time. It was 1963 before von Falkenhausen knew he was getting somewhere, when Hubert Hahne matched the score of the Jaguar which won the first European touring car championship, only losing on a technicality.

Von Falkenhausen started BMW's engines engineering department, and among the small group of technicians he gathered together to run it was Paul Rosche. A key figure in the

The poster artist catches the curves of the 328.

development of the department, Rosche would later take up where von Falkenhausen left off, bring BMW into Formula 1, and by 1975 become Technical Manager of BMW Motorsport.

Alex von Falkenhausen died in 1988, but Paul Rosche remembers the engines engineering department and its unofficial competition activities well. 'There were five designers and one person to operate the test bed. The directors were only happy if we spent no money, but von Falkenhausen encouraged us to develop racing engines as well as those that BMW could sell to the public.' Given that BMW was living through a period of commercial near-bankruptcy, the first 1500cc four-cylinder was a bold move for the department. By the time it was engaged on the Formula 1 engine in the 1980s, fifty engineers were concentrating on this one project, not counting the back-up team at the Swiss engine rebuild service.

The first car the works team was given to race was the tiny 700, the pretty Michelotti-styled Coupé with the engine at the rear. It did well to win its class in national and international races, and even occasionally startle drivers of larger-capacity cars, but the one that came to matter most was the 1500 saloon, with its tough 1499cc single overhead cam four-cylinder engine. Rosche, nicknamed 'Camshaft Paul' for his practical mathematical mastery of camshaft profiling for extra power, recalls, 'We had designed single overhead camshaft engines in every size from 700 to 1500cc – all with four cylinders and water cooling.' It fell to von Falkenhausen to persuade the management that five expensive main

bearings were necessary to support the steel crankshaft, and make a complete engine block that would be stiff enough to withstand the pressures of racing.

The BMW 1500 saloon was introduced at the 1961 Frankfurt Motor Show, but by the time the 1499cc four-cylinder reached full production in October 1962, its compression had gone up to 8.8:1 and it was giving 80bhp. But its importance as a competition engine was not so much due to its immediate success as to the family of cars between 1.5 and 2.0 litres which followed it, providing an active factory competition programme for several years.

Although most of BMW's success was on the race track, rallying did feature briefly, when Prince Alfons Metternich became 1961 German rally champion in a BMW. Good rally managers were appointed, such as Joachim Springer and Helmuth Bein, but competition over muddy surfaces rarely attracted factory support, and the Motorsport Department was usually content to leave this less glamorous side of the business to private entrants or firms like Prodrive, in Bicester, England, which was responsible for the successful rally career of the M3.

The biggest success of the M3 off the track was winning the 1987 Tour de Corse, and national rally titles in France, where François Chatriot won the 1989 series. In 1988 and 1989 Prodrive won the Belgian rally title and also finished second in the national rally championships of France and Italy.

The 1500 and its larger derivatives divided BMW's competition effort firmly into two parts: single-seater racing engines and saloon car racers. The saloon cars came first, for it was 1964 before a big enough engine was available to wrest the European touring car championship from Lotus Cortinas and Alfa Romeos.

The BMW 1800TI (Turismo Internationale) of 1963 was the basis for BMW's first 'homologation special', built to take advantage of racing regulations, and made in sufficient numbers to qualify as 'production'. It was a development of the 1773cc 1800TI officially known as the 1800 TI/SA, a *SonderAusführung* or an extraordinary sporting special. In slang it became 'Tisa' and 200 were made to homologate, or register, and qualify the model as a production car. They were diligently sold to drivers likely to use them in competition, in an effort to add lustre to BMW's reputation. For anyone who did use them on the road, there was a twin Weber carburettor 130bhp engine, 20bhp more than a standard 1800TI, and a five-speed gearbox, still relatively rare on a production car.

The 1800TI/SA propelled BMW into the competition limelight. Hubert Hahne won the German national championship in 1964, and internationally the car won three major races outright and achieved some convincing class performances. The only substantial prize that eluded it, and then only narrowly, was one of saloon car racing's best events.

The lead of the 1964 24 Hours of Spa-Francorchamps in the Belgian Ardennes was disputed over eighteen of the twenty-four hours by Rauno Aaltonen and Hubert Hahne in a BMW, and a factory Mercedes-Benz 300SE. The BMW finished second.

The following year BMW made no mistake, and won with an 1800 'Tisa' in the hands of Pascal Ickx and Gerald Langlois. It was an important victory, the first of many in this event, with its profound effect on sales in European markets, and BMW remained unbeaten in it on all but three occasions between 1973 and 1983, and again from 1985 to 1988.

The factory was also able to field the

BMWs raced in amateur and professional hands. *Top:* an 1800TISA. *Bottom:* a 2002 leads the scramble into the first corner at the Nürburgring.

1990cc (89mm × 80mm) version of the single-camshaft four in a 2000TI during 1966. Up to 170bhp and 130mph was available, and after two seasons, the works team knew as much as anybody how to keep ahead in the touring car game, which demands an inside knowledge of how to achieve a car which complies with the regulations but gives nothing away in their interpretation. The ethics of the business can be very demanding. The result was that Hahne became not only German champion but European champion as well, and BMW took the manufacturers' title for the first time.

BMW had a new European champion for the 2002, and Alex von Falkenhausen a new son-in-law, when Austrian Dieter Quester won not only his daughter Juliana but also the European titles of 1968 and 1969. The 2002 had the same slant four-cylinder engine and running gear as the 1500–2000 family, with slimmer two-door bodywork. But when the fearsome Porsche 911 arrived (it was subsequently excluded from saloon car events), BMW needed more than a competitive 2002's 210bhp.

The answer was the new, small turbochargers then becoming available. According to Paul Rosche, 'Just after Christmas 1968, von Falkenhausen told us we had to make a turbocharged engine to go racing. First we had to know what a turbocharged engine was, and when we found out, we had to discover how we make it up as fast as we can. We knew little about equipping it with an intercooler, or how to arrange the ignition controls; we just got on with it.'

Despite being restricted to 270–280bhp

on low boost and 7,200rpm, the turbo engine blew itself apart the first time it raced, the following Easter at Snetterton, in Britain. It had briefly led a 4.7 litre Ford V8, however, and proved sufficiently fast to break the opposition, and secure the 1969 titles. It was Europe's first winning turbocharged racing car, and BMW followed it up with 1,672 production 2002 turbos of 170bhp, whose debut in September 1973 made them Europe's first turbocharged cars for public sale.

BMW factory interest in touring car racing waned in the 1970s, but another firm, Alpina at rural Buchlöe, scooped the 1970 manufacturers' title using a 1600TI. Alpina also carried out development work for the racing 2800CS six-cylinder, then other specialists became involved, such as Schnitzer, at Freilässing, on the Austro-German southern border, and Broadspeed in Britain.

Although the saloons had been very successful, the BMW racing programme only really came to life with the big coupés, which did much to foster BMW's racing reputation in the more visible category known variously from 1973 onwards as Group 2, Group 5, and the World Championship of Makes.

Thus far, however, BMW had little experience of racing large cars, so it was perhaps as well that, in the spring of 1972, two of Ford Germany's key racing executives defected. They were Jochen Neerpasch and Martin Braungart, whose team of Ford Capris had been among BMW's principal adversaries. To them fell the task of putting the newly introduced BMW Coupé on a winning path.

Identifying features of the 502 of 1963, the first V-8, were foglights in the front wings, and chrome trim which set off the flowing curves of the body.

Neerpasch, a former factory Porsche driver, and Braungart, a Stuttgart-trained engineer and Mercedes-Benz rally team co-driver, brought a wealth of experience in motor racing's tricky politics, together with the highest engineering skills, and ensured there was a secure management in place when Alex von Falkenhausen officially retired in 1975.

First, the sports department was turned into a limited company within BMW. This meant it had to generate revenue of its own, which led to some bizarre money-raising activities, such as a contract (subsequently rescinded) with Ford of America to sell it 10,000 BMW turbo-diesel engines. More importantly, however, the M-for-Motorsport branding was established to sell anything from scarves to competition car assembly kits, although a longer-term significance would belong to the M-badged cars, put into production and integrated into the model range as premium-priced, faster alternatives to the standard cars.

These were created when the company offered special road cars for its works drivers to use as personal transport, in order to try out new features, or test unproven components. Hans Stuck Junior, for example, was equipped with a prototype V12 BMW Coupé in the mid-1970s. Ronnie Peterson had a succession of 3.5 litre 5-Series cars that pre-dated the launch of the 535i. These were prototypes in the sense that their drivers fed back information to the engineers on how they behaved in service — sometimes fairly vigorous service.

Peterson's reports on his 5-Series proved especially effective and led to

cars such as the M5, initially hand-made by the Motorsport Division. The first M-badged car to be sold, however, was the 165mph M1, a mid-engined coupé whose engine formed the 24-valve basis for M5 and (produced at Dingolfing rather than Munich Motorsport) the M635CSi.

For racing in the 1990s, a second-generation M5 was created with 315bhp in a comprehensively uprated 5-Series, with an M3 as part of the new 3-Series. The later M5 was manufactured at Garching, rather than Motorsport's traditional HQ at Preussenstrasse, while the M3 was built on the production line at Munich. The payroll of both Competition Department sites came to exceed 400, the majority at Garching.

Motor sport was not the chief reason for all the M-badged BMWs, only the M3 and M1 being used competitively. The M1 was a response to the Silhouette Formula proposals for Group 5 by an Anglo-German lobby in the 1970s, which found its voice as sports car racing went into one of its periodic declines.

The Silhouette Formula was for cars which looked like production cars, had to have a production-based engine, and had to have it in the same place as the production car it was supposed to resemble. It would be something of a charade, of course, and the spectators would know it was a charade, but part of the fun would be manufacturers competing with one another in a virtually no-holds-barred class of racing.

BMW took the idea on board along with Renault, Lancia, Ford, and others,

Gullwing doors open on Paul Bracq's 1972 BMW Turbo — the car that became, in essence, the M1.

Procar races supported the Grands Prix of 1980–81. Niki Lauda takes a wide line at the Rascasse hairpin on the Monaco circuit. *Above:* Near-identical cars provided close racing as the Grand Prix aces jostle with the rest.

and its 'production' model would be the CSL. Unfortunately, by the time the development of its twin-turbocharged, six-cylinder engine was complete, it had more power than a rear-drive chassis could handle. A clever alternative would be a mid-engined coupé, if only BMW had one. As luck would have it, about this time, BMW had made a concept car of just the right sort. Concept cars are made to create interest at motor shows, as an exercise for engineers and stylists, among whom was a Frenchman, Paul Bracq, working in the BMW studios.

Bracq had designed a mid-engined coupé of outstanding beauty, with upward-opening gull-wing doors. It was a car in the style of a Lamborghini or Ferrari, but with a strong BMW identity in the twin nostril air intake.

It looked perfectly splendid, so with the talent for logical practicality, to say

nothing of enlightened opportunism which, from time to time, guided BMW's hand, the demand for a Silhouette car capable of handling the CSL's turbocharged, 3.2 litre, 24-valve twin-cam power, and the Bracq design were reconciled.

Bracq's prototype had been constructed by Michelotti in Turin and was intended as a riposte to the vogue for Experimental Safety Vehicles (ESVs). Far from being tank-like, the BMW Turbo, as it was known, used a 2002 four-cylinder with a turbocharger, and had deformable structures and a jointed steering column, together with a strong roll-over bar to achieve what was known in the post-Nadar jargon as passive safety.

Yet BMW stood out for active safety, that is to say providing the driver with the best means of actively avoiding an accident rather than passively sitting

Near identical cars provided close racing as the Grand Prix Aces jostle with the rest.

waiting for it. Accordingly the car was equipped with anti-lock brakes, still something of a novelty, and its mid-engined configuration, designed to provide the best possible weight distribution, gave increased safety through superior handling.

Even after the idea of adapting the Turbo for racing had taken root, the undertaking got off to a hesitant start. Most of the engineering was done by Lamborghini, under contract to BMW, an agreement which ended in acrimony when the Italian firm was unable to complete it. There were no facilities in Munich to build the new car, named Motorsport One, or M1. However, Giugiaro, who designed the body following the lines of Bracq's car, but without the gull-wing doors, was laying down capacity for body manufacture at Ital Design in Turin, and it seemed a good idea to give him the job of making them, and supplying completed bodies to Baur at Stuttgart for final assembly. The production batch of 400 needed to

comply with the Silhouette Formula (which specified that the racing cars must look like a production model of which a minimum number had been made) was to be completed by 1 July 1979. In the event, Giugiaro was slow in getting the line laid down, and Baur and Motorsport between them made nearly all the 456 cars.

The six-cylinder engine lay amidships, running fore and aft ahead of a five-speed ZF transaxle. As a road car, the M1 had 277 horsepower, which gave it a top speed of over 160mph. In Group 4 racing trim the engine gave some 470 horsepower and, turbocharged for German Sports Car racing, 850. The M1 was introduced at the Paris Motor Show, in 1978, but the Silhouette Formula never came off, and Neerspasch was haunted by the responsibility of having created a racing car with no races to take part in.

The answer was the Procar series of 1980–81, somewhat less than dignified

BMW commissioned well-known artists to design racing livery for the 3.0 CSLs. This is the bonnet catch of the one hand-painted by Roy Lichtenstein.

supporting races at Grands Prix in which the Formula 1 drivers would, in theory, pit their skill in identical BMW M1 cars against all comers as well as each other. Inevitably, the races turned out to be cash benefits for the already well-paid world championship contenders, and the Procar championship winners were the former Brabham team-mates Niki Lauda and Nelson Piquet. The M1's best result outside Procar was when Nelson Piquet and Hans Stuck took one to third place at the 1980 1,000 Kilometres of Nürburgring.

Racing M1 with wing and air scoops directed at front brakes.

On the credit side, the result was an outstanding road car, every bit as remarkable as the 328 of the 1930s, and it did demonstrate that when it came to state-of-the-art automotive engineering, BMW had the talent and the resources to make the best. Some of the BMW management were miffed at what they regarded as a rebuff following the failure of the Silhouette Formula to happen, but it was manifestly not Neerpasch's fault. The category had become a casualty of the convoluted politics of motor racing, and not only BMW, but also other manufacturers, learned a good deal from the experience.

The foundations of M-power prosperity as an activity of the Motorsport Division were established in 1972 by Neerpasch and Braungart, when they set the engineering teams on the construction of a lightweight coupé (Coupé Sport Leicht, or CSL) along the lines of the production 3.0CS. Although publicly confident, Neerpasch and Braungart knew they were expected to win not only in Formula 2, but also against big-budget teams from the likes of Ford. To ensure big fields of BMW they

instituted a generous bonus system for private owners. The prospect of extra cash for winning encouraged outside firms such as Alpina and Schnitzer to enter their own cars, while BMW Motorsport itself ran two factory CSLs.

The racing CSLs used the production CS body shell only as a starting-point. The body panels were changed to lightweight alloy and glass-reinforced plastic, and a new engine, the M88, was laid down as a 3½ litre twin overhead cam six, with the camshafts driven by chains instead of gears, and a dry-sump lubrication system more suitable for racing. From the middle of 1973, the CSL gained the characteristic 'Batmobile' aerodynamic set of spoilers, splitters, hoops and elevated rear wings. The races were close, until Braungart and BMW developed the aerodynamics in the Stuttgart University wind tunnel which gave the Batmobiles the advantage.

Until the M88 was ready, BMW Motorsport started the season with 3.3 litre versions of the single overhead camshaft engine, developing 330bhp, which was enough to reach 167mph on the track. An Alpina BMW won the first round with only a 3 litre engine, however, thanks to the driving talents of Niki Lauda and an experienced long-distance driver, Brian Muir. Ford prevailed in the next two races, in Austria and Sweden, with Alpina and Schnitzer picking up valuable place points.

Consequently, Motorsport personnel were getting edgy when it came to their local six-hour qualifying round on the old twisty Nürburgring circuit, where the 328 had scored its first significant victory thirty-eight years before. So far,

Bizarre paintwork inspired by Greek urns extended to road cars.

Racing livery on 3.0 CSLs.
*Left*: Frank Stella's was a graphic style.
*Right*: Alexander Calder relied on large areas of colour but frequent re-touching was needed after racing accidents.

they had yet to finish an event, let alone beat Ford. This time they made no mistake: the factory cars finished first and second, Alpina picked up third, after Niki Lauda had hungrily swept to pole position in practice. He was using Alpina money to pay for his Grand Prix racing at this stage and earning all the bonus money he could. On the ageing track where he would almost lose his life four years later, he drove the daunting 14.2-mile circuit 5.7 seconds faster than any Ford could manage.

For the remainder of 1973, the CSL's winning record matched that of the BMW engine in Formula 2. Engines of 3496cc, with 366bhp at 8,000rpm, sealed the fate of the Fords, Dutchman Toine Hezemans was declared 1973 European touring car champion, and BMW also won the manufacturers' title, thanks to Alpina and Schnitzer. Most spectacular was a lap of the Spa circuit by the Amon/Quester BMW at 137.69mph, which would have been fast enough to put the car on pole position at the Belgian Grand Prix only ten years before.

The following winter, both Ford and BMW worked on new 24-valve racing engines that would yield more than 400bhp and 170mph for 1974. Alas, the series was never finished, for like so much of motor sport it fell victim to the aftermath of the crisis created by Arab oil embargoes.

Yet the BMW M49 series of double overhead camshaft (DOHC), 24-valve sixes, of which the CSL's was a prototype, had significance beyond racing. They provided a basis for an American racing challenge in the IMSA (International Motor Sports Association) series inaugurated in

1971, fully ten years before Audi imported the quattro 200s. In the longer term, these 440 horsepower racing engines also provided the basis of one of the finest in-line sixes ever in a production car. The M1, the M5 and the M635 all owe their mellow engines to that 1974 racing unit. BMW's 3.5 litre production sixes all benefited from the Motorsport engineers' faith in large-cylinder-bore racing engines.

## Saloon Car Racing in the 1980s

Changes in the regulations for 1982 made things difficult for BMW in saloon car racing. Manufacturers were now obliged to produce at least 5,000 examples of a model within a single year, to convince the authorities it was a production car. Armed with a Jaguar coupé that had been transferred into the category through something of a technicality, Tom Walkinshaw Racing almost staunched the flow of BMW saloon car racing titles, along with an unlikely ally in the shape of Volvo.

Because of low production and stricter homologation enforcement procedures in Germany, BMW was forced to race its chunky 528i saloon. With a consistent 240bhp it was able to score championship points, but it still was not fast enough to beat the Jaguar, so by 1983 a change had to be made to the 635CSi Coupés. These were developed in association with Schnitzer, and again lacked sufficient speed, because the opposition had large V12 engines (TWR Jaguar) or turbochargers (Volvo) to achieve their 330bhp. Nevertheless BMW contrived to win yet another European title with Quester.

In 1984 the V12 Jaguar XJ-S took the title, and broke BMW's run of success in the Spa 24 hours race. An angular

Volvo 240 was the 1985 winner but retired the following year after doubts about its eligibility.

Rover also withdrew, and Tom Walkinshaw Racing concentrated on sports car racing for Jaguar, leaving Ford to provide the only consistent opposition to BMW. But neither the 528i nor the 635i proved a match for the turbocharged Sierras. Some of the Motorsport staff thought the 24-valve engined M635CSi might have managed it, but the German sporting authorities (and the BMW management) agreed that production was not sufficient for homologation. Accordingly a new model had to be developed for the purpose, the M3.

Although design work began as far back as the summer of 1981, the M3 went into production in 1986 and was recognized for competition after 5,000 had been built. Paul Rosche and his engines engineers provided the M3 project team (led by Thomas Ammerschlager, former Ford Capri and Audio Quattro chassis engineer) with a highly competent four-cylinder engine which had already been adapted for Formula 2. If it was so successful as a four, would it still be as good when stretched to a six?

Paul Rosche recalled, 'Our experience with the four-valve, four-cylinder Formula 2 engine was a turning-point in the development of the six-cylinder M1 and M635. We had proved the large cylinder bore (93.4mm) for motor racing. The cylinder head design looked so good to us, that we did the first development work in two weeks by cutting up the head for a six-cylinder, and fitting it to a 2 litre four. It worked well right from the start.' It was a

Karrmann at Osnabrück made the bodies for the 2000CS, of which the back was to last longer than the front, redesigned for the 2800CS in 1968.

Racing regulations of the mid 1970s allowed a good deal of add-on bodywork. This 295 horse power Group 5 320i has wheelarch extensions to accommodate wide wheels and tyres.

versatile engine, and with the cylinders bored to 84mm it was enlarged to 2302cc, which made it suitable for racing in the 2½ litre class.

Ultimately revving up to 8,500rpm and giving around 300bhp in racing trim (320bhp under the more liberal regulations in Germany), the M3 could only have been further improved by a turbocharger, but this was regarded as too expensive to develop for the remaining production life expected for the current 3-Series car. Some 200bhp was available in the cars sold to the public (195bhp with a catalytic converter), which was enough to claim up to 146mph and 0–62mph in comfortably under seven seconds. The price in Germany was £18,500, about the same as British M3s, which were available only in left-hand drive.

As well as the 16-valve cylinder head and Bosch Digital Motor Electronics

(DME), the M3 also underwent a suspension overhaul, and gained bigger disc brakes and some clever body changes. The wheel arches were widened to accommodate 10-inch wheel rims, and front and rear aerodynamic spoilers were so carefully arranged that they complied with American bumper impact standards. The rear window and boot were given a new outline that helped keep the car steady on the racetrack at 160mph. They were modest changes – a flatter rake to the rear screen and the boot lid height raised 40mm (1.6 inches) – but they had a disproportionate effect on stability. Only racing would have provided the motive, not to mention the budget, for such detailed and painstaking research.

Once Ford was armed with the Sierra Cosworth and BMW the M3, the only world touring car championship ever run promised to be stirring. Both makes had won a title in 1987, BMW the drivers' with Roberto Ravaglia, and Ford the manufacturers' via the Eggenberger Sierra RS. It had taken the Sierra RS500 with a large turbocharger and more than 500 horsepower to do it, while BMW with its relatively simple fuel-injected 16-valve engine could manage no more than 300bhp. Yet the BMW drivers repeated their success in 1988, when the European series was replaced with the grandly-titled World Series.

After a chaotic first round in Italy, where all the leading Fords were outlawed before the race began, and all the M3s subsequently disqualified for too-lightweight body plastics, it looked as though the M3's lack of a turbocharger would be offset by better handling, and greater weight of numbers – there were plenty of private M3s ready to pick up championship points should the works cars fail.

Yet Ford still proved capable of beating BMW, through some beneficial interpretation of the regulations, which had been drawn up to allow for specification changes evolving in the course of a car's production life. These so-called evolution clauses were invoked by both sides, but Fords turned out to evolve faster, much as BMWs had while defeating Fords in the 1970s.

When the 500 'Evolution' M3s were sold to customers, they had 220bhp and the UK price was £26,960. By 1989 a catalytic converter version gave 215bhp, and there was even a special limited production series under triple BMW champion Roberto Ravaglia's signature in the UK, and that of Johnny Cecotto in other markets.
Although the RS500 Ford was

formidable competition from the middle of 1987, the M3 continued to win races and rallies not only in Europe but also in Australia and New Zealand. In Germany it remained competitive because the organizers took a lead from American racing regulations, and handicapped winners on a weight and power basis to provide close racing.

Turnover of Motorsport managing directors increased in the late 1980s. Dieter Stappert found a lucrative job guiding the sports expenditure of HB cigarettes, and was replaced on 1 January 1985 by company service specialist Wolfgang Peter Flohr, who promoted the commercial development of BMW Motorsport and the expansion of the M-badge programme. He had to face up to Ford and a home challenge from Mercedes-Benz, yet he yearned for BMW to return to Formula 1. But Grand Prix racing was still forbidden by the BMW board, and in October 1988 Flohr was replaced by Karl-Heinz Kalbfell.

## Power for Single-Seaters

Alex von Falkenhausen went to Britain for the chassis of the first single-seater BMW in 1966. He was looking for a car which would be suitable for the infamous Apfelbeck-BMW unit, for the German champion Hubert Hahne to drive. He came back with a Brabham BT7 Formula 1 chassis, which was to be followed by a number of Lola sports and single-seaters.

'I was very impressed by the new British formula cars, but the high Apfelbeck engine didn't look good in them.' Alex von Falkenhausen acknowledged that Jack Brabham's nickname for the F2 engine, 'high and heavy', was appropriate.

Everything about the Apfelbeck was complicated. It was based on a 2 litre cylinder block, with an astonishingly complex 16-valve head, and an inlet system which used eight carburettors to supply the four cylinders. It was designed by the Austrian motorcycle speedway expert and experimental engineer, Ludwig Apfelbeck. The valves were disposed radially, with the inlets and exhausts opposite each other instead of side by side, as on most four-valve heads, and needed intricate porting systems on opposite sides of the engine. It needed not only two complete induction systems, but two separate exhausts as well.
'The complicated valve drive with rockers was not good for high revs. The 1600cc engine for F2 had terrific problems, but the 2 litre was much better because it didn't rev so high,' according to von Falkenhausen.

Details of the heads were kept secret for a long time – cynics suggested it was because BMW thought nobody would believe they could ever have fallen for such a bizarre scheme. Whatever the truth, when the Apfelbeck worked, it delivered significant horsepower – 225bhp at 9,500rpm, 140.8bhp per litre – on highly explosive Nitromethane mixtures, but often to the accompaniment of truly operatic tantrums.

The Apfelbeck flattered with some promising performances in hill-climbs and both von Falkenhausen and Hahne tested the car at Hockenheim, where von Falkenhausen set the record for the standing start ¼-mile and 500 metres – his last competitive appearance. It also did 111mph for the standing kilometre, but it was an achievement as notable for its speed as its short duration.

The Apfelbeck proved to be a blind alley, along with the innovative 'Diametral' BMW-engineered unit, in which the inlet and exhaust valves were diametrically opposite one another, and complicated the head design still further by using three spark plugs per cylinder.

'Apfelbeck was very angry when his head was discarded. He never accepted it and felt his engine must be better than the later one. Rosche was a designer at BMW and I discovered that he was very good, so after Apfelbeck left, Rosche took over.'

The engine was not, alas, BMW's only mistake. Another was commissioning a racing car chassis from Dornier on the other side of Munich. The designer, Len Terry, complained that Dornier kept putting holes in the stressed-skin structure, weakening it, and when he was recalled as a consultant to restore the ride height, he solved the problems by having it made more precisely in accordance with his original intention.

These forays of the 1960s developed from weekend hill-climbs and record exploits, into an attack upon the first European Formula 2 Championship of 1967. This single-seater category was the last step before young drivers made it into Grand Prix racing. The engine rules attracted BMW by calling for production cylinder blocks, of 1.6 litres at first, 2 litres from 1973.

By 1976, teams would be allowed to use pure racing designs which no longer needed to be derived from a production engine, attracting V6s from Renault and Honda. Between 1967 and 1972, the Ford-financed Cosworth FVA was almost unbeatable, especially

The Apfelbeck, the controversial engine which took BMW into single-seater racing.

when it was mounted in cars designed by the leading Grand Prix teams such as Lotus, Matra and Brabham. BMW sometimes had more power, up to 225bhp on 10,500rpm, but beyond 9,000rpm the Apfelbeck tended to self-destruct.

It was not until 1970 that Jacky Ickx won a Formula 2 race for BMW. The Motorsport Division had first to adopt a twin overhead camshaft and 16-valve combustion chamber arrangement similar to the Cosworth, but there was no loss of face in applying somebody else's principles. BMW had reserves of goodwill in the bank; it had already had enough good ideas of its own, which other people had copied, to allow reciprocity on an occasion like this.

Besides, the team had acquitted itself honourably enough with the ill-starred Apfelbeck. BMW came close to winning the 1969 title for non-graded drivers (primarily those who were not in Grand Prix racing) with their own engine and the Dornier-BMW chassis designed by Len Terry. The team had also suffered its share of tragedy, when Gerhard Mitter died in a Dornier-BMW at the Nürburgring in August 1969.

Neither Hahne nor Siffert won a race outright, but Hahne was first non-graded driver home. In 1970 the long-awaited success arrived. With a formidable team of Ickx, Siffert, Quester and Hahne, the Dornier BMWs won four races and Quester lay fourth equal in the European championship with Ronnie Peterson. But BMW Managing Director Paul Hahnemann forbade more racing.

'Just when we started to become

successful, they decided to stop. I don't know why – perhaps it was just to show his power,' von Falkenhausen complained bitterly. 'So, at the last race, the Neubiburg airport race at Munich, we took big black cloths and covered the cars. The newspapers printed this funereal picture and the board was very, very angry.'

Despite the ban, von Falkenhausen kept on racing. His son-in-law Dieter Quester had bought a March 712 chassis and they used a 1970 engine which should have stayed at the factory, but somehow escaped. In the event the March chassis was much better than the Dornier, and Quester finished third in the European championship behind Ronnie Peterson and Carlos Reutemann and ahead of Niki Lauda.

Formula 2 racing glory began properly in 1973, when a change in the regulations admitted a notable BMW competition engine. Designated the M12/6, it was a comparatively simple 2 litre four-cylinder with a slightly stretched bore (89.2mm), a standard 80mm stroke, and mechanical fuel injection from Kugelfischer. Double overhead camshafts, with cam profiles developed by Paul Rosche, added to

BMW single seater of 1970, 240 horse power three-valve per cylinder engine, Len Terry-designed, Dornier-built hull.

the bite of an engine that only came into its own well beyond the safe maximum rpm of its production counterpart. Installed in a March 732, painted in the bright dayglo red of the STP sponsor, the M12/6 gave Jean-Pierre Jarier 275bhp at 8,500rpm and a chance at last of consistent success.

Jarier won eight of the seventeen qualifying rounds to become 1973 champion in a season when BMW overcame the Ford-Cosworth by thirteen races to four. It was also the season that the big BMW Batmobile coupés finally beat the V6 Capris, not only giving BMW substantial cause for celebration, but also marking another stage towards its return to the front rank of prestige car manufacturers.

A modified M12/7 engine brought European Formula 2 titles for Patrick Depailler in 1974, and Jacques Laffite in 1975. It was really a different Schnitzer version, but the BMW block remained intact. By 1978 it was the turn of an Italian driver, Bruno Giacomelli, to take the European title for BMW and March again, while the following season it was the Swiss, Marc Surer, giving BMW the opportunity to promote itself in each driver's home market.

The final F2 title came against the fiercest opposition, with Corrado Fabi winning against the impressive Ralt-Hondas in 1982. Celebrating their tenth year of racing together, March and BMW won eleven races against Ralt-Honda's three. Fabi scored five victories and more championship points than his March team-mate Johnny Cecotto, later a frequent winner with the M3.

Modern Formula 2 racing lasted some seventeen years, from 1967 to 1984, when it was replaced by the 3 litre F3000. The last two seasons, including a poorly supported final year, fell to Ralt-Honda, and BMW-powered cars won twice. March-BMW and Christian Danner finished third overall through consistency and reliability rather than speed.

Formula 2 served BMW not only well but profitably, for Motorsport sold more than five hundred racing engines. Factory engineers had competed against the best in the world – ideal training for Grand Prix racing when it came. Detail development, particularly around his cherished camshaft profiles, allowed Paul Rosche to reflect, 'By the close of Formula 2, the average maximum power had risen from 275 to 315bhp, or 157.6bhp a litre. The best we ever saw was 321bhp, and the normal maximum power zone was 9,500 to 10,000 revs: the final evolution version (M12/7/1) gave best power on 10,200.'

Such figures are impressive enough to engineers, but a more telling endorsement of the performance was a test of the 305 horsepower Formula 2 car in 1978 by the late Manfred Winkelhock. This showed that it had the same 0–100mph acceleration as a contemporary twin turbo racing Porsche 935. The German *Sport Auto* magazine revealed 0–62mph in 3.5 seconds (against 4.6 for the Porsche), 0–100mph in just 6.6 seconds, and little more than ten seconds was needed to reach 124mph.

According to Rosche, 'Formula 2 gave us a basis for a lot of other projects.' These included technology transfers to the production car side in the M3. 'The experience was very important to us, and I had a lot of fun, and did a lot of hard work with the people at March in England. The four-cylinder was developed in turbocharged form, first for saloon car racing, and then, as the M12/13 series, we found that it had the potential to be made ready for Grand Prix racing.'

**The Road to Formula 1**

An image-building programme had been in progress for the production 3-Series car, to make it the logical follow-on for the highly regarded 2002. The sports department decided to turn it into an international racing project, with factory support in America as well as Europe. Its objectives were limited, and nobody really foresaw that it was going to provide BMW with the data for an engine that would fit into a Grand Prix car, and provide the power and reliability with which to win the world championship.

The 3-Series racing cars for the production touring category were radically modified parodies of the 320i, conforming to the regulations known as Group 5, which restricted competition managers' imagination hardly at all. It demanded only the outline of a production model, and an engine in its production location. BMW used the faithful M12/7 Formula 2 power unit, yielding slightly over 300bhp, together with a Getrag 5-speed competition gearbox and racing suspension based on the CSLs.

The shape of the car was developed with help from Pininfarina's wind tunnel. The body was a shortened version of the production shell with steel panels inside, wings, spoilers and glass reinforced plastic covering the wide

wheels. Both balance and cooling were improved by side radiators.

The running gear could, and in the longer term did, absorb double the original horsepower, and required only detail changes during its racing career. Over thirty were sold to private racing teams at more than £30,000 apiece, some to America, where the plan was to take on Porsche again, and produce a car that might win world championship Group 5 races outright. In any event it put BMW back in the turbocharging business with a 2.1 litre stretch of the versatile four.

McLaren at Livonia, Michigan, USA, and their associates in Britain, such as Nicholson McLaren Engines at Colnbrook, were given the job of redeveloping the Formula 2 engine, and adding the turbocharger. They made it capable of winning American races, with 620bhp, by means of a Garrett AiResearch installation at a pressure of 1.3 bar.

Despite lowering the compression from 8:1 to 7:1, the engine's limiting factor in Europe was a high incidence of piston failure, due to the lower octane petrols specified by the racing regulations. It was never a long-distance competitor for the Porsches, yet, without its turbo, it was a near-certainty for class honours in the world and German championship seasons of 1977 and 1978.

America was also the backdrop for BMW's most serious sports racing effort yet, namely McLaren North America running a BMW GTP that proved capable of winning, and reaching 210mph. It was dogged by misfortunes, however, including fiery failures of its BMW Motorsport turbos, but when it was running it was giving up to 800bhp at 9,000rpm.

BMW also supported the car that won the 1978 German championship. The Schnitzer 320 of Austrian Harald Ertl confirmed the potential of the four-cylinder in turbocharged trim, at a capacity close to the new turbocharged class emerging in Grand Prix racing. Josef Schnitzer, the team's original driving force, died in 1978, but the co-operation with BMW survived, and another piece of the Formula 1 jigsaw fell into place.

The Formula for Grand Prix racing specified cars with 3 litre engines, or 1½ litres with a supercharger. From its inception in 1966 the 3 litre Formula, as it was usually called, was just that. Nobody made a supercharged car of 1½ litres because so much of its power would be absorbed in running the supercharger.

Renault was the first to spot the possibilities of what might properly be called turbosuperchargers, in which a tiny turbine is set spinning at prodigious rpm by the exhaust gases rushing through the downpipe. Turbochargers effectively give something for nothing, creating extra power by forcing more air into the cylinders.

It was a principle that was not lost on aircraft engine designers, where the problem is lack of oxygen at high altitudes. By putting in more air under pressure, they supplied the engine with more oxygen. But the means of doing so – superchargers – needed engine power to run them. Turbos bought the extra power cheaply by making the heat and pressure and the speed of the outflow down the exhaust pipe, that

The aggressive prow of the 1970s BMWs later appeared insensitive, and was changed.

would otherwise go to waste, drive a turbine to turn the supercharger.

Based on the competition 320i, the engine had to be reduced in size to 1426cc, to come inside the regulations for the 2 litre class when turbocharged. It had a KKK (Kuhlne Kopp & Kausch) turbocharger, and developed 410bhp (287.5bhp a litre) at 9,400 revs. Paul Rosche recalled, 'The Schnitzer car of 1978 was so interesting that we got behind the 1979 GS Tuning 320 that was being prepared for Markus Höttinger. 'When BMW started to apply more serious boost (1.5 bar) and modified the engine's breathing, it produced 610bhp, more than enough to be competitive in Formula 1. Clearly, there was material here for a Grand Prix engine – all that was missing was the decision to go ahead and make it.

### At last – Formula 1

In some ways the Grand Prix engine came about in a manner uncharacteristic of BMW. A Grand Prix project from the firm had often been predicted, but when it did occur, it was through a series of unrelated events rather than a carefully plotted path. It was to be Germany's first Grand Prix motor since the 1.5 litre Porsche of the early 1960s, yet it nearly became bogged down in political difficulties within the company. It was to be a very protracted birth.

Jochen Neerpasch was still in charge, but he was in disagreement with his ambitious deputy, former motoring journalist Dieter Stappert, over a suitable destination for a BMW Grand Prix engine. Neerpasch, an ardent Francophile, had given his word to the Talbot Sport organization that they should have it. Stappert and many of

the Bavarian sports staff disagreed. There was plenty to argue over, and a good deal of lobbying in related departments of the main office, within a few minutes' walk of Preussenstrasse.

It was Stappert and his supporters, including the directors of sales, engineering and public relations, who prevailed. By November 1979, Neerpasch had left, and in February 1980 Stappert confirmed that serious development work had begun on the project, and he had become the new BMW Motorsport Manager, a position for which Neerpasch had groomed and recommended him. Spring 1980 saw the BMW management tear up the Talbot Formula 1 engine supply agreement, and on 8 March BMW said they would give it to Brabham alone.

Three key factors were in Brabham's favour. There was already a good working relationship with BMW-contracted drivers Niki Lauda and Nelson Piquet. Secondly, there was the power and influence of the Formula One Constructors' Association (FOCA), which lay largely within the grasp of the then Brabham owner . Bernie Ecclestone, who had played a leading role in the M1 Procar series. Finally, there was deep admiration at BMW for the talent of the Brabham designer Gordon Murray.

Paul Rosche recalled that the technical parameters for the Grand Prix unit were rapidly established, but making it work within the aerodynamically demanding confines of a Formula 1 car was a challenge. 'We always knew we would use the four-cylinder, and when we saw that the Höttinger 320 engine would stand over 600bhp, our job was to develop what we already had become

World Champion Nelson Piquet, Paul Rosche of BMW, and Brabham designer Gordon Murray.

familiar with, through years of Formula 2 and saloon cars.

'We stayed with the usual production 89.2mm bore. At Motorsport we took the 56mm stroke crankshaft of the Höttinger project to 60mm, with titanium for the connecting-rods, to give 1499cc. The compression started at 6.7:1 and boost was around 1.8 bar for 570bhp, but of course these things varied between test, qualifying and race sessions.'

The first track tests, at Silverstone on 13 October 1980, saw a suitably modified Brabham BT49, with a BMW engine producing 557bhp at 9,500 revs. The car appeared in public for the first time on 18 July 1981 in practice for the British Grand Prix, but although it was fourth fastest, it was not raced.

Brabham preferred its well-tried Ford-Cosworth V8s for too long in BMW's view, so that it began to look as though the team lacked confidence in the BMW engine. Exasperated, the following April BMW issued an ultimatum, threatening the end of further co-operation with Brabham unless the engine was raced.

The result was a formidable alliance. The driver with most faith in a project that had looked uncertain in its early stages was Nelson Piquet; the BMW turbo engine fitted his hard-driving style, and he used every bit of his world championship-winning talent during his BMW testing, development and racing days. And just to show how difficult the task was, the engine's first victory came one cool Canadian evening, after Piquet and the Brabham had failed even to qualify for the Detroit Grand Prix the previous weekend.

There were some difficult times when neither competitive nor reliable performances came from the engine and the Anglo-German alliance was visibly stressed. The amiable Stappert needed all his diplomacy to keep the BMW management and the robust Brabham racers from falling out. The respect of Paul Rosche for Murray's profound abilities also held the team together.

Paul Rosche had difficulties of his own. 'At the beginning we had Bosch-Kugelfischer mechanical fuel injection and the twin intake KKK turbocharger, but things changed a lot over the racing seasons. We were after more power, but we were also looking for durability. The regulations eventually restricted turbo boost, which put a four-cylinder at a disadvantage against V6 twin turbos. They could rev higher to get better power under boost control, and with two banks of cylinders, their exhaust pulses to the turbos on each side were more frequent. To begin with, the power was coming in at between 7,500 and 10,500 revs, and we increased this to 11,200, putting us very near the point at which the engine would literally blow itself to pieces. One

Nelson Piquet in the Brabham BT52 won three Grands prix in 1983, came second three times, winning the championship narrowly from Alain Prost in a Renault.

missed gearchange and that would be it, whereas the V6s were happy running to 12,000rpm and more.'

The highest horsepower obtained from the BMW Formula 1 engine depended on the regulations, which tended to change from year to year. Practice engines, which were deemed expendable, gave more power than race engines, which had to last the full distance. Rosche estimated that from a starting-point on low turbo boost of around 550bhp, an all-out peak of more than 1,000bhp was obtainable. 'Our test dynamometers do not read any higher.' In 1983, when Piquet won the world championship, with an extra-large KKK turbocharger, the engine regularly gave 640bhp at 11,000rpm.

In 1984, Motorsport proved that an increased compression (7.5:1) together with 3.9 bar boost would release a racing-reliable 950bhp, but at the time a lot of failures were attributed to fuel composition, so it was difficult to say how trustworthy the engine really was. Official power quotes were 100bhp less, probably closer to the truth in fuel economy conscious 1985, when 900 to 910bhp was more usual.

The rpm peak power quote was extended to a doubtful 11,200 in the unsuccessful 'lay flat' engine era for Brabham, when a specially low-built car proved a very demanding installation. Outputs of 1,050 to 1,100bhp were expected for qualifying engines which, according to Rosche, 'allowed a driver to go all-out for a good practice time for a maximum of two laps, by which time the engine would be completely destroyed.'

Such were the extremes to which the

humble production 1500 cylinder block was put.

The cubic capacity and major components remained much the same throughout BMW's involvement with Formula 1. From 1980 to 1982, BMW factory engines were supplied only to Brabham, whose contracted drivers were 1981/83/87 world champion Nelson Piquet of Brazil and Riccardo Patrese of Italy.

In 1987, its last season as the official BMW M12/13 engine, it was still rated around 900bhp at 11,200rpm, but BMW was now less happy about its competitive state, as the regulations restricted boost to no more than a sustained 4 bar. Yet there was more to the fund of knowledge obtained by the racing engine than experience with turbocharging. Rosche felt afterwards that the development of Bosch Motronic engine management systems that could be applied to production engines was an even more important result to come out of the years of effort.

By 1983 the German-owned ATS team had gained BMW supplies for their driver and BMW contractee, Manfred Winkelhock, and until their withdrawal as a factory engine supplier at the close of 1987, BMW continued to supply Brabham. At different times ATS, Arrows at Milton Keynes in England, and, for one season each, Benetton (1986) and Ligier (1987) were also supplied with BMW turbo power units.

By the time it came to racing the new engine, Lauda had retired (for the first time), and it was Piquet who set second fastest practice time in the first race outing, South Africa on the weekend of 23 January 1982. The race itself was not

Arrows kept the BMW flag flying in Grand Prix racing, but the day of the turbo was over.

a successful debut for Brabham-BMW and Piquet: aside from unreliability, the engine had very abrupt power surges which made things difficult for the driver, until the Canadian Grand Prix later in the season.

Of BMW's nine Grand Prix wins, Nelson Piquet scored seven, and of the fourteen pole positions (fastest practice times) recorded by BMW engines, Piquet set eleven. Brabham team-mate Riccardo Patrese inherited a South African victory as Piquet-slowed to make sure of the 1983 title, and the final BMW-powered Grand Prix win went to BMW protégé Gerhard Berger and his Benetton B186 in the Mexican GP, 1986.

BMW officially withdrew from Formula 1 engine supply at the close of 1987, but its techniques lived on in the upright four-cylinder turbocharged Megatron engine serviced by Heini Mader in Switzerland, an engine that served the 1978/88 Arrows equipe at Milton Keynes.

Certainly Rosche and his engineers

could look back with satisfaction to the high turbo boost era of Formula 1, when they were able to challenge the best in the world and beat them. For the late 1980s BMW saw its priorities as producing and engineering its road cars, and its racing was confined to the production-based saloons it had always supported with such success.

Yet the final credit for the great 1500 belongs to the late Alex von Falkenhausen. Most engineers would have been happy to have such an engine as a career epitaph, but von Falkenhausen did not regard it as his greatest achievement. 'The six-cylinder was most satisfying. Of course a four-cylinder can never be made as smooth as a six. But this six was smoother than any other and remained so.' The pride of an engineer exemplified. His directors were pleased too.

'When our BMW directors met the Daimler-Benz directors once, the Daimler directors said "We think our cars are better except in one thing. You do a better engine" From this moment I was very popular.'

The decision to revive the old pre-war numbering system was taken in 1972, the year the Olympic Games came to Munich, and a huge sports stadium was built on the site of the old airfield where the BMW story began. The stadium grew on the opposite side of the Munich ring road from the soaring new headquarters building, known as the *Hochhaus* to most Müncheners, but as the *Vierzylinder* (four cylinder) to the architects, anxious as ever to draw visual analogies. Alongside was built a vast bowl, inspired by the Guggenheim Museum in New York, with a spiral deck inside to house displays unfolding the BMW view of the world and its place in it.

The three principal model lines emerged in distinct phases. In 1972, the 5-Series was launched, in 1975 the 3-Series and, in 1977, the 7-Series. All of them were subsequently revised and relaunched, but this was the establishment of the pattern of three strong divisions catering for distinctive segments of the market. The 6-series cars were essentially coupés which borrowed components liberally from 5 and 7, but were sufficiently different to take on an identity of their own. The 8-series for the 1990s, however, had a number of distinctive features which set it apart, almost as a fourth string to BMW's bow.

The plan was that the 5-Series would form the core of the range, a middle-class car competing head-on at last with its Mercedes-Benz counterpart. In 1972 it was still a four-cylinder, still single overhead cam, still only 2 litres, and while the handling was good, the emphasis was more on speed, style and comfort than straightforward

## DRAWING

## THE

## LINES

The rear end of Wilhelm Hofmeister's 2000cs coupé of 1965 survived the transition to the first of the three later coupés of 1971.

## Das Cabriolet der Neuen Klasse
Aus Freude am Fahren. 85 PS. Von 0 auf 100 km/h in 13,3 Sekunden. 160 km/h Spitze.

Floppy tonneaus still covered folded hoods in the 1970s. By the 1980s, the customers demanded button-down metal lids.

sportiness. The appearance was tidied up, while still recognizably related to other BMWs, and the interior was carefully laid out, with instruments in a new glare-free housing lit at night with a red-orange glow.

Within a year, the 520 was joined by a six-cylinder, the 525, and in 1975 the 528. Soon every second BMW sold would have a six-cylinder engine. Following the logical pattern of model numbering, these were 5-Series 2.5 litre and 5-Series 2.8 litre, in the same crisp four-door, three-box saloon body shell, with a distinctly forward sloping front, like the prow of a ship – fashionable, but not too avant-garde. BMW did not want to change the expensive body dies too often, so the designers chose a style which would weather the winds of changing fads.

It was the firm's view that its customers were a fairly conservative lot, easily offended by anything fancy. The 5's proportions were good, and its most distinctive feature was four headlights embraced by a single panel, with the traditional BMW grille, which proved astonishingly adaptable to modern shapes, neatly placed in the centre.

One of the stylistic clichés against which BMW stood out was large areas of glass. The uniformity of the BMW line remained important, and the firm was not interested in trimming decimal points off the drag coefficient at the expense of comfort by allowing strong sunshine to overheat the interior through big windows.

Gerd Hack of *Auto, Motor und Sport*, one of Germany's leading motoring magazines, put it succinctly: 'Why should a car consist of so much glass? It is not the styling that makes so much heat inside; it is the uncontrolled use of a material that technically speaking has disadvantages for a car. Glass is more expensive, heavier, and more dangerous in a crash than metal.'

The broad grille and the clipped lines of the 5-Series.

The 5-Series replaced the so-called New Class car that had put BMW back on the road to prosperity; it was the first car to be produced at the old Glas plant in Dingolfing, an hour's drive down the valley of the River Isar from Munich, and it was, for its time, large and roomy. In 1977 it became related to the 3-Series when the 520 gained a 2 litre, six-cylinder engine from the 320. Another pattern was established – that of overlapping engines between the 3s and 5s, and the 5s and the 7s.

Between 1972 and 1981, 700,000 *Fünfers*, as the 5-Series came to be known, had been made, and a new version arrived. It looked fairly similar to the old one, rounded off, tidied up, better aerodynamically, but still readily identifiable and still not, according to BMW publicity, knocking the bottom out of the second-hand values of the existing cars. Keeping the appearance much the same was a policy that disheartened enthusiasts, but it probably made commercial sense.

Production of the 5 went up by 30 per cent within a year of the new car's introduction, despite difficulties in export markets for large cars – France put a special tax on them, while Sweden and Switzerland made technical demands which meant building special models for those markets.

The arrival of the new 5 also meant a reduction in the average fuel consumption of BMWs by six per cent, following an undertaking to lower the consumption of the entire range by 15 per cent before 1985. The revised 735i of 1982 used no more fuel than the 318i automatic had in 1978. When electronic controls were applied to the turbocharged 745i engine-transmission package for the first time, consumption was reduced by ten per cent.

Almost alone in the industry, BMW's sales were hardly affected by the fuel crisis, although the company hedged its bets with the introduction, in January

1975, of the 1502, with a low-compression 1.6 litre engine in the old-style body. The future of large cars with their heavier fuel consumption remained in doubt for some years after 1973, when the price of oil increased by 70 per cent virtually overnight following the Arab-Israeli October war. The Arab countries cut production in protest against the United States' support of Israel, and the world was plunged into the oil crisis which convulsed the world of motoring.

The first edition of the *Fünfer* arrived on the market just in time for what came to be known as the first oil crisis, for there were more shocks to come. In Britain, petrol ration books were printed for the first time since 1956, and the repercussions of the event brought about the closure of two hundred of the nation's petrol stations. In January 1974, in the fourth rise inside twelve months, petrol went up to 50p a gallon.

Elsewhere in Europe, speed limits were imposed. In Holland and France, rationing was introduced; cars with odd-numbered licence plates could only be used on odd-numbered dates, those with even numbers only on even-numbered dates. There was a brisk trade in small cars as families with odd-numbered cars looked for second cars with even numbers in order to remain mobile. Weekend motoring was restricted in an effort to conserve the supplies of petrol that were coming through. There seemed to be no ceiling to what drivers were prepared to pay in order to keep running, but soon it became clear that the crisis was not a temporary phenomenon. The days of cheap energy had gone for ever.

The upward pressure on fuel prices

remained long after the direct consequences of the 1973 war had disappeared. And there was another problem looming – pollution. Since the 1950s, when cars were found to cause the photo-chemical smog that plagued the Los Angeles basin, changes had been on the way. Emission control regulations came into force in California in 1968, and the rest of the United States followed two years later.

Controls became stricter in 1983, but even progress towards clean lead-free exhausts could not disguise a change in the way fast cars came to be regarded throughout the world. Demand for catalytic converters grew, but they could not alter the fact that when cars are driven fast the pollution they create increases.

It took time for the market to settle down after the first oil shock. Mercedes-Benz hurried plans through for a smaller car than it had been making hitherto because, like other manufacturers, it had to acknowledge that the sudden increase in prices, while political in nature, had an underlying rationale, namely the finite nature of the world's oil reserves. The future for large, thirsty cars appeared bleak.

It would be some years before discoveries of larger reserves of oil than anybody suspected, such as those in the North Sea, provided reassurance. But ever larger and faster cars would never again be regarded with quite such equanimity.

Accordingly, the arrival of the first proper 3-Series, the 1802 in 1975 as the successor to the old '02' cars, the 2002, 2802 and 1602, was opportune. Once again BMW kept the strong family

An early BMW small six. Smooth engines were to be an enduring characteristic of the make.

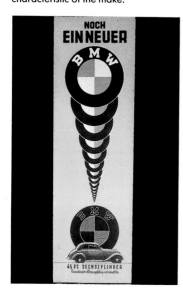

resemblance to the cars they replaced, but shrewdly the new body was changed enough to keep it modern, without following fashion too closely.

BMWs of this era still looked smartly contemporary; it is only with hindsight they seem rather passive and unadventurous. Their style did not wear as well as that of, for example, the Jaguars of the period, which continued to look elegant and in vogue long after they went out of production. Modishness was something that BMW was content to avoid, although whether this was due to a clear act of policy or, as seems more likely, to a combination of circumstances is a matter for debate.

The 316, 318 and 320 of 1975 were all four-cylinder cars; from 1977, the 320 and 323i gained the new generation M60 sixes of 122 and 140 horsepower, giving these relatively small, two- and four-door saloons with their 100-inch wheelbase a lively turn of speed. They could accelerate briskly to 120mph. Yet the distinguishing feature of the new six-cylinder cars was their capacity for smooth, quiet operation, a characteristic for which they were naturally suited because of the equilibrium of a six-cylinder engine, in which the crank throws and ignition intervals occur every 120 degrees of crankshaft rotation, and balance one another out.

The principal novelty of the M60 was a belt drive for the overhead camshaft, although the old chain-driven four-cylinder engines continued even when the replacement 3-Series came out for 1983. Over 1.3 million of the old model had been made – over 3 million if the previous similarly-sized range was included. This was another design

which disappointed enthusiasts when it appeared, because yet again BMW had replaced it with something which looked pretty much the same as before.

In point of fact, none of the old body panels remained the same. The change was almost complete, but it had the appearance of a warmed-up version of the old car, at a time when rivals were producing radically different styles, and some of the customers felt short-changed. BMW, it seemed, was not trying hard enough.

The 1983 revision of the 3-Series made the company appear more conservative that it probably was. A current fad, not to say obsession, was with Cd, or coefficient of drag, a measure of aerodynamic efficiency, which was expected to be close to the Audi 100's 0.30 to be any good at all. It was not a very satisfactory benchmark; the important criterion was really frontal area. The Cd figure was only a measure of how well the aerodynamicist had done, given a frontal area of so many square metres. It was not an absolute guide of how fuel-efficient a car was, but nevertheless a slippery look was in vogue, and BMW's rather blunt angularity began to look a little passé.

Yet aerodynamics had not been ignored. On the new 3, they were improved mostly by detailed changes, such as making the windows nearer flush with the body sides. Conflicts arose between the requirements of the engineers, to whom wider-section, low-profile tyres were essential because they so improved the roadholding, and of the aerodynamicists, to whom they were anathema because they affected the Cd figure badly.

The button-down hood of the 3-Series (top), and the rounded 5- and 7-Series, short of the aggressive prow, moulded for the 1990s.

*Overleaf:* The Z1, dramatic lines and, like the 328, a re-invention of the sports car.

Satellite tracking. High performance cars made by Alpina, an out-station within BMW's orbit. *Left to right*, B10, B6, and B12.

The effect was unspectacular. The 3-Series could get no lower than 0.38, even though it looked more slippery. Despite its slightly downwards-sloping belt-line, which gave it a fashionable wedge shape, the boxiness remained. Still, the customers liked it, and the second-hand market liked it, which sustained residual values and, claimed BMW, reduced the cost of owning one, which had been its aim all along.

The engineers won the battle over wider wheels. They needed to, however, because the 3-Series was not the only latter-day BMW to suffer from sudden, sometimes treacherous oversteer, or tailheaviness, that could snap the back of the car away on a wet road with startling speed . The problem was tackled on the new 3-Series by changing the angle of the trailing-arm rear suspension (still, in principle, the old faithful from the 700) from 20 degrees to 15 degrees. This reduced the camber, or lean, of the tyres, on bump and rebound. It was the old problem that used to afflict the pre-war swing-axle cars in another form. The tyres were not keeping their tread

square-on to the road surface, and when they lost grip, they did so suddenly.

By the 1980s, BMWs were already being constructed largely by robots, which helped keep the quality consistent. The computer-controlled arms welded the body together with great accuracy, allowing the production engineers to cut their coat, as it were, more economically according to their cloth. This was done not so much to save on steel as to reduce body weight. Using robots to weld tighter body seams took 8½ per cent off the weight of a 3-Series car.

The new techniques also improved rust-resistance, and allowed a six-year anti-corrosion warranty to be offered – a response to the rival Audi's fully galvanised body. BMW's improvements also made the cars quieter, better insulated, and an on-board computer was employed on all models right down to what might be regarded as an entry-level BMW. It monitored safety-related items such as failed bulbs, oil, water and washer reservoirs, with warning lights in a panel above the windscreen.

The debate about whether cars should be hand-made or engineered carefully enough to provide the advantages of craftsmanship without its drawbacks, was resolved at BMW by careful production engineering. Cars stopped being hand-made because a better alternative was found. Hand-made cars could proceed no farther beyond the state of the hand-made art, while robot-made cars could, and did.

BMW doors were a case in point. When a 5-Series body was made, the door openings were measured by lasers and surface scanners. The doors fitted into the openings with the sort of accuracy only a computer-controlled system could achieve. There was no filing bits here and bending pieces there afterwards; there was no need. No filler was added, nobody had to make a judgement on how well things *appeared* to fit.

The door hinges were welded in place, not screwed into pre-drilled holes as by most manufacturers to allow for adjustment later. There was no error, so there was no need to make room for error; it was a question of the confidence of the engineers. The doors aligned perfectly, and clicked precisely shut, the seals filling the gap to exclude draughts, noise, wind and water. The result was better than anything a coachbuilder could achieve, and likely to last much longer, not sag or come loose – short of a major accident.

Build quality at BMW meant such attention to detail. In case of an accident, the 5-Series was equipped with bumpers that were exchangeable deformation units – impact boxes with hydraulic dampers, that deformed and prevented damage to the engine supports in collisions up to about 10mph. They were easy to exchange and relatively simple. The boxes so reduced the cost of repairs that the later 5-Series cars were rewarded with a lower insurance group rating.

In the 1980s BMW became sensitive about speed. All the petrol-engined 5-Series cars could manage over 200kph (124mph), and the company issued a statement saying, 'Top speed is not an objective in itself. Rather, this superior performance is only a

by-product of the cars' power and efficient streamlining.' What this meant was that BMW was adhering to an agreement among some German manufacturers not to emphasize speed, and to limit the fastest models to 250kph (155mph).

The car this affected most was the 7-Series. The first one was introduced in 1977, replacing the 2500 and its derivative 2800 which had been the firm's large car since 1968. The styling carried over the understated conservative idiom of the 5-Series; details were important in what was effectively the spearhead to the challenge to Mercedes-Benz, with a touch of polished wood inside, a tidy toolkit in the bootlid and, for the United States market, the name Bavaria.

The name in particular took a trick. It gave the car a strong identity and marked the arrival of BMW into North America as a major force. Bavaria nameplates were even acquired privately by owners in other markets for the *cachet* they carried. Once again much of the car's prosperity lay in its splendid six-cylinder engine, a great

Special equipment for the 535i, a sporting wing and spoiler to tidy the aerodynamics.

heart for what *Car & Driver* described as a top-of-the-line sedan at a middle-of-the-line price. BMWs were not invariably sold at a premium figure. Even at its best, BMW would never account for more than one-third of one per cent of the United States market. They were never going to be thick on the ground.

The US was never plain sailing for BMW. At the beginning of 1980, the dollar sank to DM1.70 and middle-of-the-line prices became a thing of the past.

When the 7-Series was announced in 1987 – the 728 with 2788cc and 170bhp, 730 with 2985cc and 184bhp, and 733 with 3210cc and 197bhp – the style for BMWs of the 1980s began to emerge. Only the 733 was sold in North America, and it was to gain a distinction which paralleled that of the 328 sports car in the 1930s, bringing together assets hitherto regarded as irreconcilable. It showed that the virtues of a sports sedan could be combined with the luxury of a limousine.

The 733 had variable power steering that adjusted itself according to need – plenty of push at parking speeds, less when the driver needed good feel of the road when driving faster. It had a check control panel, through which electronics monitored the car's systems, plus electric windows, air conditioning, a supple ride, and refinement, without compromising the good handling and spirited performance for which BMWs were so notable.

In 1978 came the 635CSi, which would run for the best part of twelve years. This was a notably well-proportioned coupé, based on the 5-Series, and would last well past the introduction of

the next 5-Series in 1988, which was being planned throughout yet another threatened interruption to the world's petrol supply.

In June 1979, coinciding with a mid-term re-launch of the 7-Series, the Organization of Petroleum Exporting Countries (OPEC) raised its prices once again, not by the large margin of 1974, but by a still hurtful 24 per cent. In 1982 they cut oil production by 2½ million barrels to 18 million. In the face of an oil price of $34 a barrel, it needed strong nerves not only to continue the development of a completely new six-cylinder, 3.4 litre 7-Series, but to proceed with the design of BMW's most ambitious engine yet, the aluminium 5 litre V12. As the price of petrol in Germany went up to over 1DM a litre for the first time, the outlook for a large saloon of well over 300 horsepower was not promising.

After the first oil crisis, BMW had decided to produce its own diesel, but by the time the low-revving eta-engine was available, early in the 1980s, fuel was once gain relatively cheap, and a slow BMW seemed out of place. Product planning, so important to any company but fundamental to car production, was becoming a matter for the clairvoyant and not just the well-informed. Even so, BMW stuck to a policy of eight to ten year model cycles in contrast to the shorter and shorter lifetimes of American and, in particular, Japanese cars.

BMW needed all its good head of steam. It was the fastest-growing car company in Europe in the 1970s, lying sixteenth in the turnover league table and, when production reached half a million cars a year in 1989, fourteenth in

The tail light clusters of the M1 were standard production BMW items. The bodies were made by Baur in Stuttgart with designer trimmings.

the volume stakes. Inside ten years, sales had doubled, turnover increasing fourfold. A decision had to be taken to carry on with the 7-Series, a flagship car in keeping with the aspirational nature of BMWs throughout the world. There had to be a BMW at the top of the tree towards which the 3-Series and 5-Series customers could aspire, or the whole marketing structure would be incomplete.

BMW marketing was based on a number of well-established assumptions about BMW buyers. Research suggested they were successful executives, often self-employed, well-educated and high-earning. Many of them started with a second-hand BMW, or the numerically prominent 3-Series, and moved up in due course as they got older and more prosperous. And while it was clear that fuel economy was going to remain important, BMW reasoned that even a large car could be provided with an acceptable petrol consumption, thanks to fuel injection (standard on the 7-Series since 1979) and modern engine management systems.

There was pressure from the German Government to improve fuel consumption in line with the United States' mandatory Corporate Automotive Fuel Efficiency (CAFE) regulations. BMW Chairman Eberhard von Kuenheim had to reassure the German Research Minister, Volker Hauff, that BMW was paying attention. Between 1970 and 1980, the number of BMW research staff working on fuel economy and environmental issues generally increased threefold.

Research was not confined to cars for the immediate future. BMW in the 1980s became one of the most advanced automotive firms in the field of hydrogen-propelled cars, and in 1987 was able to demonstrate to the politicians in Bonn that they were also well ahead in electric cars. In collaboration with Brown Boveri, a sodium sulphur battery was developed which weighed 265kg, worked at 300°C and, in a 3-Series body, could do some 100km between recharges.

It was run experimentally with an ordinary 12-volt battery to provide the power for accessories such as the radio, and a small furnace which burnt old-fashioned hydrocarbon fuel for heating the interior.

The hydrogen project looked more convincing. A long-term programme of research aimed at adapting the internal combustion piston engine to work on hydrogen demonstrated that it was a practical proposition. The benefits of burning hydrogen were clear: it produces no carbon dioxide, no hydrocarbons, only oxides of nitrogen and water. The problem was how to store a sufficient quantity within the compass of a car safely.

To be compressed into a space roughly the size of a petrol tank it had to be liquified, which meant designing a double-walled vacuum superinsulated container and keeping it at minus 250°C. After that, it only required an extra water injection system to make it burn in the cylinders rather than explode; it could even be switched from petrol to hydrogen without much ado. BMW's experimental hydrogen-fuelled cars were fully licensed and insured for the road.

All that was needed was the hydrogen

BMW flagship, the 7-Series. The kidney-shaped grille is flatter on the six cylinder, wider on the similarly-bodied V12.

farms in the desert to make the necessary quantities without using up existing energy resources.

The 3, 5 and 7 were traditionally made in roughly the proportions 65, 25 and 10 per cent, varying as models neared the end of their cycles, which BMW liked to sustain at around ten years. Until the new 5 in 1988, the 3 was important in volume and profit terms, the 5 gradually catching up to 40 per cent, the 7-Series to more than one BMW in ten. The exclusive 6-Series and later the 8-Series coupés had a different role, catering for customers who might otherwise defect from BMW towards Porsche or Mercedes-Benz and set, from BMW's point of view, a bad example to colleagues.

This was a strategy that unfolded in the 1970s, with the Quandt family well in control of BMW. They had come on the scene in the late 1950s, when the firm was losing money, and frustrated banks were ready to sell it to Daimler-Benz. They bought a large minority stake, paving the way for the 60 per cent they would acquire later. Herbert Quandt had chosen a former machine tool company executive from Hanover, the cool, urbane, softly-spoken Eberhard von Kuenheim, to run the company in 1969, and in BMW's tradition of long-serving principals, he stayed. Following the example of Franz-Josef Popp, who joined as the Austrian Government representative in 1916 and remained until the Nazis forced him out in 1942, von Kuenheim saw the company from the 1960s into the 1990s.

Quandt money gave BMW the opportunity to survive and press on with the development of new cars such as the important mid-range model, the 1500 of 1961. Two years later the company was able to pay its first dividend for twenty years, a pattern that would endure throughout the next quarter century and beyond.

By the beginning of the 1980s, BMW's sales in America were climbing dramatically; 40,000 in 1981, 50,000 in 1982, and nearly 60,000 in 1983. Japan was penetrated for the first time. Home sales, 130,000 in 1982, continued to rise despite a damaging metal-workers' strike between May and July 1984. Sixty thousand BMWs were lost then, of which 35,000 were only regained by workers doing without holidays and coming in to do extra 'recovery' shifts.

By 1988, BMW's success was putting pressure on Daimler-Benz to bring competitive cars into production, and von Kuenheim could never quite disguise his satisfaction. 'Daimler-Benz is such an excellent company and we have such respect for its achievements that we regard it as an honour when we are compared with them,' he said.

**The Z1's plastic body panels are detachable from the fully galvanised steel chassis. The floor is made from a moulded sandwich of epoxy resin and foam, which will not rust.**

By the dawn of the 1990s BMW's turnover was DM20,000 million, ten times what it had been in 1970, and it employed 63,000 people. Take-over talk had surfaced from time to time, and

was never taken lightly, but the prospects of it diminished as time went on. Several times the Quandts had to make it clear they did not want to sell, and von Kuenheim was happy to back them up. The Quandts had, according to the Chairman, given the company 'a certain consistency', although the success of the company rested on years of steady and patient effort.

It was this patient effort that renewed first the 7-Series in 1986, then the 5-Series in 1988, then the Z1 and the 8-Series, and finally brought the new 3-Series into being as the last decade of the twentieth century broke. BMW plants at Regensburg, Munich, Dingolfing, Lower Bavaria and Steyr contributed to a prosperity that BMW had not seen since the 1940s and as each model took the road, it was regarded as a pace-setter, a benchmark that other manufacturers tried to emulate.

In the construction of the Z1, BMW took a leaf out of Rover's book. Twenty-six years earlier, the Rover 2000 came out with its body panels bolted to a skeleton frame, a system which promised better quality production and easier repair after accidents. BMW re-invented it and refined it for a remarkable new sports car every bit as advanced for the 1990s as the 328 was for the 1930s.

The Z1 was displayed as a prototype in mid-1986 by BMW's highly specialized 'Think Tank' department, BMW Technik. It was hardly an affordable sports car in the style of the MG Midget; the sports two-seater had grown into an expensive and complex car. Despite a high target price of DM83,000, customer reaction was good enough to

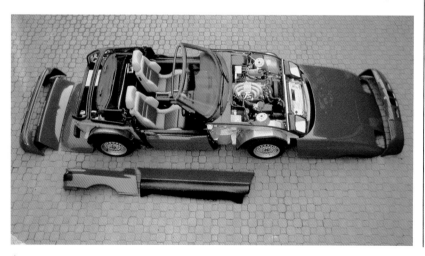

The El Spider, BMW's study for a car of the Twenty-First Century shows a Z1 styled for the next generation. Aircraft-style electronics enable it to cruise at 155mph on computer-controlled highways in safety.

persuade BMW to begin production in 1988 at the low rate of six cars a day.

Only thirty cars were scheduled to be imported to the UK market in the first year, yet even at £40,000 apiece and deposits with orders, BMW(GB) soon had 75 customers ready with their cheque-books. In the event, production was slower than expected – not for the first time in BMW's history.

Yet the Z1 was far and away the best-handling and most secure-roadholding BMW of modern times, largely thanks to a new rear suspension later incorporated into the new 3-Series. It performed well, with a 140mph top speed, and reached 60mph in around 8 seconds – not quite a match for a Porsche Turbo, but swift enough to keep up with most hot hatchbacks.

Not having a roof tends to make an

open car literally sag in the middle, but the Z1 was built on a stout, fully galvanized pressed steel structure, and instead of the Rover's steel and aluminium body-cladding, the Z1 was provided with plastic panels of, for a sports car, unusually high aerodynamic efficiency.

The clean quality of the aerodynamics could be demonstrated by driving it fast with the top down. The slipstream barely ruffled the driver's hair.

The Z1 marked BMW's return to the truly sporting league from which it had been absent since the 1930s. It was a car that re-wrote the specification of the sports car much as the 328 had done. The days of BMW as an aero-engine manufacturer may indeed be gone, but BMW motorcycles still occupy their special niche, and BMW cars have their unique qualities that make them well worth a celebration.

*Overleaf*: Coupé class. Seven generations of BMW coupés from the 1930s to the 1990s. Right to left; 327 1937–41, 503 1956–59, 3200 CS 1962–65, 2000c 1965–69, 3 litre CS 1968–75, 635 CSi 1976–89 and in the foreground the 850i, BMW's coupé for the 21st Century.

# ACKNOWLEDGEMENTS

An author is only the executive tip of an iceberg of individuals who put a book together, and my thanks are due to many. Chris Willows not only gave permission to quote from an invaluable interview he obtained shortly before the death of Alex von Falkenhausen in 1988, but also gave the book much encouragement and aid, well beyond the call of his duty as Public Affairs Manager of BMW (GB). Lorna Arnold and Scott Brownlee of the PR Department at Bracknell were also most helpful in the long process of finding things out and ensuring their correctness. BMW's racing history fortunately has a chronicler who can be relied upon, so I sought Jeremy Walton's help in tracing the developments which led up to the single-seater triumphs of the 1980s. Frank Page, a keen motorcyclist himself helped greatly in researching the motorcycling chapter. BMW keeps a large storehouse of priceless archives in Munich, and kindly agreed to give me access to them and put me right on a multitude of BMW detail. My thanks are due to Peter Zollner, in particular for his lucid explanation of the ingenious Kommandogerät, convincing evidence that BMW inventiveness did not begin with the Z1. George Halliday of BMW Archiv would allow no inaccuracy in his kindly reading of the manuscript but had to put up with some differences of emphasis, and Frau Strothjohann found obscure photographs with great patience and much charm. Book editors have a not altogether thankless task, because authors are bound to thank them. I do so in the heartfelt way an author does when a book is finished; to Gillian Young and Joanne Rippin, much thanks. Credit must also go to sources, in particular Horst Mönnich, whose monumental official history of BMW is an invaluable foundation on which to build. Finally my thanks are due to my publisher. Colin Webb, my agent Lucinda Culpin of the June Hall Agency and the Peters Fraser and Dunlop Group, my secretary Joyce Horley, and most importantly my wife Ruth and my family, for sharing the anxieties of authorship. I promise to make it up to them.

Andrew Yeadon's pictures appear on the following pages:
1, 2/3, 6/7, 9, 10/11, 12, 18/19, 25, 28/9, 34/5, 36, 38/9, 44/5, 50/1, 56/7, 62/3, 67, 72/3, 75, 76/7, 83, 84/5, 92/3, 99, 100/1, 104/5, 106, 109, 113, 115, 116/7, 122/3, 129, 132/3, 138/9, 144/5, 151, 158/9, 166/7, 169, 172/3, 176, 178/9, 180, 181, 183, 186.